Joseph Priestley (1733–1804) was one of the great intellectual figures of the English Enlightenment and also one of its outstanding political theorists. His discussion of 'civil liberty' is crucial to understanding the debates that swirled around the War of American Independence and the Dissenters' bid for wider religious toleration. His response to these events was informed by his central commitment to a natural right to 'freedom of thought'. Despite the fundamental importance of this concept in modern political thought, Priestley's role in its articulation has been ill-served by the absence of a modern edition of those works in which the argument was forged. This new collection will be the first to make accessible to students Priestley's *Essay on the First Principles of Government* and *The Present State of Liberty in Great Britain and America*, which reflect his most concentrated engagement with these issues at a crucial moment in his own life and that of the state. An introduction and notes, together with guides to further reading and key figures in the text, provide the student with all the material necessary for approaching Priestley.

CAMBRIDGE TEXTS IN THE
HISTORY OF POLITICAL THOUGHT

———

JOSEPH PRIESTLEY
Political Writings

CAMBRIDGE TEXTS IN THE
HISTORY OF POLITICAL THOUGHT

Series editors:

RAYMOND GEUSS
Professor of Political Science, Columbia University
QUENTIN SKINNER
Professor of Political Science in the University of Cambridge

Cambridge Texts in the History of Political Thought is now firmly established as the major student textbook series in political theory. It aims to make available to students all the most important texts in the history of western political thought, from ancient Greece to the early twentieth century. All the familiar classic texts will be included but the series does at the same time seek to enlarge the conventional canon by incorporating an extensive range of less well-known works, many of them never before available in a modern English edition. Wherever possible, texts are published in complete and unabridged form, and translations are specially commissioned for the series. Each volume contains a critical introduction together with chronologies, biographical sketches, a guide to further reading and any necessary glossaries and textual apparatus. When completed, the series will aim to offer an outline of the entire evolution of western political thought.

For a list of titles published in the series, please see end of book.

JOSEPH PRIESTLEY

Political Writings

EDITED BY

PETER N. MILLER
Clare Hall, Cambridge

CAMBRIDGE
UNIVERSITY PRESS

CAMBRIDGE UNIVERSITY PRESS
Cambridge, New York, Melbourne, Madrid, Cape Town, Singapore, São Paulo, Delhi

Cambridge University Press
The Edinburgh Building, Cambridge CB2 8RU, UK

Published in the United States of America by Cambridge University Press, New York

www.cambridge.org
Information on this title: www.cambridge.org/9780521425612

First published 1993

A catalogue record for this publication is available from the British Library

Library of Congress Cataloguing in Publication data
Priestley, Joseph, 1733–1804.
Political writings / Joseph Priestley; edited by Peter N. Miller.
p. cm. – (Cambridge texts in the history of political
thought)
Includes bibliographical references and index.
ISBN 0 521 41540 3 (hardback). – ISBN 0 521 42561 1 (paperback)
1. Political science–Early works to 1800.   2. Liberty–Early
works to 1800.   I. Miller, Peter N.   II. Title.   III. Series.
JC176.P86   1993
323.44–dc20   92–27753 CIP

ISBN 978-0-521-41540-8 hardback
ISBN 978-0-521-42561-2 paperback

Transferred to digital printing 2009

FOR HERBERT FRIEDMAN

Contents

Acknowledgements	*page* x
Introduction	xi
Chronology of Joseph Priestley's life	xxix
Biographical guide	xxxi
Bibliographical guide	xxxv
Essay on the First Principles	1
The Present State of Liberty	129
Index	145

Acknowledgements

A community of thinking people, whose creation Priestley thought so fundamental to life well lived, is rarely of greater value than when preparing something for publication. The editors of this series, Raymond Geuss and Quentin Skinner, have been of tremendous assistance. Martin Fitzpatrick's great expertise saved me from misstatements and Simon Schaffer read an earlier draft of the introduction. I am grateful to D. O. Thomas for answering queries at various stages in the life of this project. Naomi C. Miller helped me recognize the degree to which reformers such as Priestley were interested in and informed about European affairs such as the debate over toleration in Poland. Many thanks to Richard Tuck, though this time for his skills as a literary sleuth. Rich Connors, Alan Cromartie and Anthony Milton answered political, linguistic and ecclesiastical queries with grace and aptitude. They have my thanks. A version of the introduction was read to the eleventh Le Moyne Forum on Religion and Literature, where it benefited from the comments of Richard Ashcraft, Jonathan Clark and John Pocock. Once again, it is a pleasure to thank Brian Jenkins, Christine Fenn and the staff of the Rare Books Room of the Cambridge University Library for their consistent help and assistance. Richard Fisher and Nancy-Jane Thompson have been lots of fun to work with and have made dealing with Cambridge University Press very pleasurable. Finally, this book is dedicated to one of America's greatest astrophysicists – and uncles – who, for as long as I can remember, has shown me by example what great pleasure there is in intellectual enquiry.

Introduction

Political thought in eighteenth-century Britain reflected the circumstances of a post-revolutionary society. In the first half of the century
the need to legitimate the Revolution of 1688 and its twin products,
the new regime and the new British state, shaped the structure of
political argument. In the second half, the increasing friction within
the empire and the renewal of a demand to increase the extent of
religious toleration introduced new themes and new stresses.
Together, the colonial rebellion and the French Revolution were to
pose the most severe challenge to the usefulness of the conceptual
language of 1688.

Because the distinction between the person of the sovereign and
the power of sovereignty was still being delineated in early modern
Europe, and because it was (and remains) easier to generate loyalty to
a person than to an abstraction, an altered royal succession under-
mined the foundations of obedience. The flight of James II and his
replacement by William and Mary meant that the re-establishment of
secure loyalty, last faced in England after the execution of Charles I
and the creation of the Commonwealth (1649), was the chief political
priority. In the immediate aftermath of the Revolution, its defenders
and opponents debated questions such as the legitimacy of resistance,
the legalities of succession, the power of Parliament and the rights of
kings. The unwillingness of a small but vocal section of the population
to take the requisite oaths of loyalty emphasized the lack of consensus.
Stout defenders of the spiritual and temporal role of the Church of
England, so-called 'High Churchmen', denied that the divine right of
kings could be trampled upon by Parliament. The right to resist even

a king was upheld on the grounds that the monarch's authority derived from his obligation to secure the common good; his failure to do so deprived him of that authority. Over the course of the eighteenth century this claim, which was the basis of 'Revolution Principles', was turned against those Whigs in power by those out of power. These latter included not only disgruntled or excluded politicians, but a smaller core of writers who broke with the ruling circle, or 'junto', as early as the 1690s because of their view that modern Whiggism was irreparably flawed. These have been termed the 'true' Whigs or 'Commonwealthmen' because of their allegiance to the 'good old cause' of Milton and Harrington. Where outright tyranny had once constituted a monarchical threat to the public good, they believed it was now imperilled by the insidious practices of parliamentary corruption.

Supporters of government and opposition each claimed that they were more patriotic than the other, in other words, that they were possessed of a more powerful commitment to the welfare of the community. This domestic debate was transformed by the consequences of an international confrontation. The management of Britain's empire rarely entered into discussions of corruption or patriotism before the middle of the century. Even those few writers who warned of potential problems tended to view national and imperial politics as separate spheres.

The Seven Years War (1756–63) changed all this. Discussions of the state of the empire had tended to focus on the means of enhancing its commercial value. But the addition of Canada and India meant that the managers of the empire had now to cope with a physical reality that posed different questions. Fundamentally, commercial empires were expected to be financially self-sufficient, paying for themselves through exports to the mother country. Territorial empires, however, aside from requiring a more substantial and therefore expensive administrative and military establishment, were so large as to vitiate the economic relationships that made them profitable. Hence the British decision, in 1763, to introduce a series of colonial taxes to pay off some of these costs. The subsequent dispute over colonial taxation, recognized at the time as a debate over the location of sovereignty in the empire, quickly assumed the contours of a challenge to the basic notion of representation that had justified the supremacy of Parliament, and especially of the House of Commons, in Great Britain. Those 'friends of America' who had taken up their cause in speech, sermon and pamphlet were not slow to recognize that the lack of adequate representation complained of by residents of Virginia and New York was an equally legitimate cause for complaint in Manchester and Liverpool – though it was precisely this injustice that had been held up by the government and its supporters as a sign that colonists were not singled out for maltreatment. Fundamentally, the crisis of the empire in the third quarter of the century made clear that the Atlantic Empire was no single community and therefore could have no single common 'good'. Since individual policies, as well as the Revolution itself, were constantly and perhaps inevitably justified by appeal to a common good, this devastating colonial claim called into question not merely imperial administration, but the very basis of the eighteenth-century British state.

The argument that individuals determined their 'common' good in a concrete fashion by electing representatives was in fundamental conflict with the contemporary practices employed to control Parliament. The existence of property qualifications limited the size and characteristics of the electorate. The legal manipulation of borough charters and the installation of placemen, or government dependants, in safe seats limited the choice of Member of Parliament to those deemed acceptable to the ruling party. Demands to break the grip of this electoral control were blocked by identifying reform with the seventeenth-century civil war.

Among the British supporters of the colonial position were many latitudinarian Anglicans and dissenters. Behind the colonists' demand for representation lay the conviction that the notion of 'consent' had to be redefined to suit the new circumstances of a continental empire separated by thousands of miles of ocean from the metropolis. The prominence of the individual in this new argument corresponded with the latitudinarians' and non-conformists' long-standing demand for the end of subscription to the Thirty-Nine Articles of the Church of England and the repeal of the seventeenth-century Test and Corporation Acts. Oaths of loyalty to the ecclesiastical establishment, like those to the civil establishment, remained a source of friction. Moreover, those who refused to subscribe to these fundamental articles of the Church of England were excluded from a variety of public offices. The defenders of a reciprocal relationship between church and state relied on the received view that the stability of the state was enhanced by the civil enforcement of religious uniformity. Objections were raised on the grounds that there could be no justification for civil intervention in affairs of individuals beyond what pertained to their civil status. It was this coincidence of claims for colonial representation and broader toleration in the writings of James Burgh, John Cartwright, Richard Price and Joseph Priestley in the 1770s that provided the conceptual foundations of, and set the agenda for, the parliamentary reform movement of the next half-century.

Because of their broadly similar political and theological orientation these men have usually been examined in the context of investigations into later eighteenth-century English Radicalism. Our appreciation of this political culture can, however, be deepened by recognizing what actually separated these reformers from one another. Of them all, Joseph Priestley's contribution to this new discourse was profound, immediate and distinctive. Born into a Calvinist family, his education at the dissenting academy at Daventry led him into a career in the ministry and education. As a lecturer in history, languages and *belles-lettres*, Priestley must have been revolutionary. He drew upon a wide range of sources including legal codes, archaeological remains, linguistics and coins in order to provide concrete accounts of past societies. Although now famous for his scientific endeavours, most notably the discovery of oxygen, Priestley's natural philosophic efforts began as an avocation.

His adoption of the Socinian belief in the humanity of Jesus (increasingly being called Unitarianism) underpinned a basic commitment to the capacity of human beings to understand the world through investigation. It was, in fact, a defence of intellectual enquiry that drew Priestley into the political and ecclesiological debates of the later 1760s and formed the nucleus of his most complete statement of political thought, the *Essay on the First Principles of Government*. Priestley's circle of friends in the early 1770s, the club of 'Honest Whigs', included leading dissenters, supporters of the colonies, and famous colonists, including Benjamin Franklin. Through the interventions of his friend Richard Price, Priestley gained appointment as librarian and scholarly confidant of the Earl of Shelburne in 1772, in whose circle at Bowood he and Jeremy Bentham first met. In 1780 Priestley decamped to Birmingham where he returned to the pulpit, taking up a post as minister. He now pursued his scientific investigations with great vigour in the midst of another society of creative minds: the famous Lunar Society of Derby, whose number included Erasmus Darwin, Josiah Wedgwood and Thomas Boulton. Priestley's support for the French Revolution led to increasingly heated verbal attacks and, ultimately, the catastrophic riot and sack of his home and laboratory. Emigration to America seemed to offer the only escape from a political climate that had grown increasingly inhospitable.

In his own lifetime he gained national and international fame as a writer on electricity and pneumatic chemistry. Priestley was elected a Fellow of the Royal Society and was warmly received by Franklin's Philosophical Society in Philadelphia after he emigrated. Perhaps the closest parallel to be drawn, in terms of breadth of interest and ability, is with Franklin. Priestley's celebrity must not be underestimated: upon disembarking at New York he was greeted by the Mayor of the City and the Governor of the State. Upon reaching Philadelphia two weeks later he was received by President Washington.

There are three basic divergences between Priestley and his fellow reformers ('radical' being both misleading, since they perceived their aim as reform, and anachronistic, since the word was only coined in the 1790s). Priestley's intellectual interests were far wider, his moral philosophy came to rest on a different foundation and his political interest was more limited. First, his intellectual interests, as reflected in a vast written *oeuvre* – more than 150 books of which many are multi-volume, along with countless letters and sermons – span the wide range of disciplines that we now associate with the greatest of eighteenth-century polymaths and *philosophes*: history, literature, linguistics, rhetoric, theology, moral and political philosophy, and the contemporary versions of psychology, chemistry and physics. A work entitled 'Joseph Priestley in Context' would, even more than most studies of its kind, far surpass the competence of any single chronicler.

In addition to Priestley's exceptional breadth, the first problem faced by any investigator is that posed by the fundamental change in his thought in the 1770s. A survey of Priestley's career that fails to acknowledge this dynamic quality can only mystify. Until approximately 1772 Priestley's published works reflect the influence of Samuel Clarke's moral philosophical interpretation of Newton's natural philosophy. Newton's God was omnipotent, omniscient, benevolent and self-moving; Clarke had employed the famous Analogy between created Nature and the moral world in order to derive from these divine attributes the image of the individual as an intelligent, rational and, most crucially for questions of moral agency, free creature. These are the premises emphasized in the moral philosophy of James Burgh (*The Dignity of Human Nature*, 1754) and Richard Price (*Review of the Principal Questions and Difficulties in Morals*, 1759). Priestley's contribution to this genre, *The Institutes of Natural and Revealed Religion* (3 vols., 1772–4) actually engages critically with the inheritance of Clarke. This is an important divergence between Priestley and the other reformers. *The Institutes* seems poised between his friends' philosophy of moral liberty and his own subsequent plunge into materialism and increasing fascination with the theory of 'associationism' derived from the work of David Hartley. In Volume I (1772) Priestley described an almost Clarkean divinity characterized by 'Power, Wisdom and Goodness', but no longer by self-motion or liberty. From 1775, when he issued an edited version of Hartley's *Observations on Man* with three appended essays, these views were systematically renounced: the Newtonian division between passive matter and active principles was replaced by the union of Matter and Spirit, and liberty was vitiated by a materialist reading of Hartley's associationism even more determinist than Hartley's own.

What was the consequence of this clear allegiance to Hartley's system of thought? Most obviously, Priestley could no longer campaign for philosophical or intellectual liberty on the grounds of its correlation with actual human liberty. Liberty could be advocated only as part of a project to bring about the perfection of God's world, one in which the fulfilment of the divine plan, rather than human action, was important. Priestley's language of natural rights has less and less in common with the conventional usage; this marks a parting of the ways between Priestley and his fellow-travellers of the late 1760s and earlier 1770s. This may help explain the increasingly millennarian tone of his political writings in the subsequent decades. Hence also the published debate with his good friend Richard Price, with whose views Priestley's are often conflated. *A Free Discussion of. . . Materialism and Philosophical Necessity* (1778) deals with exactly these questions about the possibility of human liberty. Precisely because Price drew heavily on the particular discussion of liberty initiated by Clarke, Priestley's disagreement marks his divergence from this common origin.

The third important distinction that needs to be drawn within the circle of reformers reflects the relative importance each assigned to politics. For Burgh, Cartwright and Price, the crisis of the empire highlighted the necessity of reforming the state. Burgh argued for an extra-parliamentary national association and Cartwright spent the next fifty years organizing just such movements for parliamentary reform. Price's most famous tract was called *Observations on Civil Liberty and the Nature and Justice of the War with America*, making plain his view that reform of the state and of the empire coincided. In addition, Price took a leading role in the petition for the repeal of subscription to the articles of the Church of England and abolition of the Test and Corporation Acts. At no stage, however, did the colonial problem play a fundamental role in the shaping of Priestley's thought, nor, despite his literary contribution, did he seek active involvement in the political fight for toleration.

The relationship of Priestley's political thought to that of his contemporaries and friends can be clarified by appreciating the circumstances out of which it emerged. In the preface to the first edition of the *Essay on the First Principles of Government* (henceforth *Essay*) Priestley wrote that the treatise had its origin in the urgings of his friends to expand on 'the remarks I formerly wrote on Dr Brown's proposal for a code of education' (*Essay*, p. 3). Brown's *Essays* on Shaftesbury's *Characteristics*, as well as much of his poetry and dramatic writing, all pre-dated his two tracts on political, social and moral decay: the fantastically successful *Estimate of the Manners and Principles of the Times* (2 vols., 1757–8) and *Thoughts on Civil Liberty, on Licentiousness and Faction* (1765). Brown's argument in this, and in an appendix to the contemporary sermon *On the Female Character and Education* (1765), was that the reformation of morals essential to the preservation and flourishing of the community, required that the States take an active role in the education and upbringing of children. This was the argument that drew Priestley's fire in *An Essay on a Course of Liberal Education*, which he then acknowledged as the nucleus of the *Essay*, and which was reproduced in its entirety as Section IV, 'In what manner an authoritative code of education would affect political and civil liberty'.

Over the next decade Priestley's political writings sought to describe an alternative to Brown's model of the relationship between government and individuals. This argument, not the actual situation in North America, motivated the articulation of his political thought.

Hence the basic division between the structure of his major theoretical treatise and those of Burgh, Cartwright and Price.

Priestley was not, however, oblivious to contemporary events. His *Present State of Liberty in Great Britain and her Colonies* (1769) drew the conclusion that political conditions in both halves of the empire constituted a threat to the liberties of Englishmen. This argument may have been a model for the later writers. Furthermore, in passages inserted into the expanded second edition of the *Essay* (1771), after the implications for Britain of the debate over imperial representation had been made clear in the ever-expanding occasional literature on the colonial crisis, Priestley attacked septennial parliaments and the levying of taxes on unrepresented colonists. Other additions amplified the claims for the primacy of the individual in the formulation of policy laid out in the first edition. Still, Priestley's politics of reform remained a product of his response to Brown. It was driven by a perception of human intellectuality, of the use and life of the mind, with the content of civil liberty and the determination of the just bounds of government following from this description.

The opening sentence of the *Essay* states the premise of the work. 'Man derives two capital advantages from the superiority of his intellectual powers.' Prudence and the capacity for improvement are characteristics of human beings and, therefore, had to shape the structure of social life. A long passage omitted from the second edition clarifies the position of Priestley's argument. Intellectual growth enabled the individual to distinguish between present and future needs; prudence, therefore, was set against any crude utilitarian calculations. From this followed the book's central theme and greatest innovation. Brown shared with many other early modern theorists of the state, both republican and monarchist, a strong sense of the political centrality of some notion of the 'common' or 'public' good. In fact, Brown was himself an admirer of Spartan society, which mandated a harsh subordination of the individual to the claim of security. Priestley did not reject the concept of a 'public' or 'common' good altogether, nor did he deny that it was in some sense a measure of policy, but he did differ from Brown and the bulk of his contemporaries in his way of defining the content of that good, and he set narrow limits to the area within which it could claim pre-eminence. In particular, actions by the civil ruler that were incompatible with the satisfaction of the real needs of individuals, even when such actions were ostensibly directed at the pursuit of the common good, could rarely, Priestley thought, be justified.

Priestley's discussion of the nature of individual liberty was elaborated in opposition to Brown's infatuation with Sparta, and, in particular, Brown's claim that its constitution demanded the enforcement of rigid intellectual uniformity. In Priestley's words, this would have put 'an effectual stop to all the noble improvements of which society is capable' (*Essay*, p. 117). Priestley explicitly challenged Brown's two central claims, that freedom of thought could be restricted in the interest of national security, and that Sparta was an example of a state that had benefited from such a policy. Priestley's alternative sought to meet Brown on his own ground, and so was also couched in the idiom of 'ancient' politics. What Brown had lauded as Sparta's greatness was in fact her backwardness. Priestley denied that the duration of a state, a fundamental principle of ancient politics in its early modern adaptation, ought to be a measure of political success. The longevity of a state that 'secured to a man the fewest of his natural rights' was not a goal to be sought. Here Priestley's own agenda, the desire to promote individual intellectual improvement, collided with the commonwealth concern for the integrity of the political life of the community. Thus, the same priorities that led him to reject Sparta led him to a revaluation of the exemplary status of ancient Athens. Despite its 'convulsions', life there was better precisely because there was a possibility of intellectual exploration, even if attended with some political instability (*Essay*, p. 109). The 'arts of life' as they flourished in Athens offered the possibility of 'governing ourselves like men' while the anti-intellectual Spartan system amounted to the governance of 'brutes'. Self-government depended on intellectual development and not constitutional arrangement. Because of this emphasis Priestley was prepared to accept a degree of diversity of social purpose that went far beyond that of Brown – or even of less strident 'commonwealth' writers. 'The various character of the Athenians was certainly preferable to the uniform character of the Spartans, or to any uniform character whatever' (*Essay*, p. 45).

Brown had thought himself the 'true enemy of sedition' and wrapped himself in the language of contemporary patriotism. Priestley's reformulation of the purpose of social life led him to redefine patriotism as well. The 'true' patriot was one who 'proposes, with a manly freedom, whatever he thinks conducive to the greatness and glory of his country' (*Essay*, p. 127). Here Priestley has completely subverted the classical republican understanding of *gloria e grandezza*. Its content is no longer the result of war but of thought, and its perfection the consequence of 'indulging unbounded liberty and even caprice in conducting it' (Priestley, *An Essay on a Course of Liberal Education* (henceforth *Liberal Education*), London, 1765, p. 147).

The priority of intellectual enquiry excluded the possibility of political solutions based on a fixed canon of historically deduced maxims, since any attempt to freeze social and political arrangements would soon be undone by the 'progress' of the mind. 'Were the best formed state in the world to be fixed in its present condition, I make no doubt but that, in a course of time, it would be the very worst' (*A Course of Lectures on the Theory of Language*, Warrington, 1762, p. 192; also *Essay*, p. 109). The possibility of 'improvement' stated at the outset of the *Essay* is repeatedly invoked against schemes that would have frozen the condition of individuals. Government was 'the great instrument of this progress of the human species' and could not, therefore, impose conditions that would retard or eliminate improvement. Priestley repeatedly emphasized that even the most well-intentioned moves to limit change were wrong. The actual history of the Protestant Reformation and the related changes in the nature of religious worship provided Priestley with his strongest argument for the claim that change was usually for the better, since the body most resistant to change, the Church of England, was itself the chief beneficiary of just such an alteration scarcely two centuries earlier. Because the practice of natural philosophy was fundamentally characterized by this notion of improvement and exploration it provided Priestley with a ready alternative to Brown's attempt to derive specific policies from the past. Since 'what ever depends upon science, has of late years been in a quicker progress towards perfection than ever', he argued that social life could expect similar gains were individuals left more or less unencumbered (*Liberal Education*, p. 162).

Priestley believed that while it was true that 'Unbounded free enquiry upon all kinds of subjects' could result in some 'inconvenience', its restraint produced 'infinitely greater inconvenience' (*Liberal Education*, p. 177). 'Inconvenience' was an important term for Priestley as it determined the legitimacy of state intervention in the mental and physical lives of its citizens. Where

John Locke's influential argument for religious toleration had sought to preserve a space for the individual conscience by distinguishing between the purview of civil and religious authority, Priestley recognized that a civil ruler could always claim that his intervention was warranted because religion was inevitably a political issue. While conceding that 'all claims of individuals inconsistent with the public good are absolutely null and void', he dissented from the standard assertion that it consisted in the security and preservation of the community. Precisely because Priestley had a view of human nature that emphasized intellectual progress he was able to argue that the good of a society composed of intelligent creatures actually made government intervention in all but the most obvious cases of assault on 'the lives, liberty or property of the community' inadvisable. Thus, in *The Present State of Liberty in Britain and her Colonies* (henceforth *Present State*) he declared that 'the good of the whole' required the subordination of individuals to the community only 'with respect to those things in which the public can make better provision for them than he could for himself' (p. 134).

Instead of this common belief that the more mankind was governed by the 'united reason of the whole community' the better, Priestley argued that, on the contrary, greater 'inconvenience' would follow from such practice. As an alternative, Priestley suggested that the extent of government be determined by its effective performance. Where 'numbers', or community, aided the individual's pursuit of his or her good then government intervention could be warranted – but in no other instance (*Essay*, p. 30).

Freedom of thought was the paradigmatic illustration of the limited value of 'numbers'. While Priestley granted that 'more discoveries' would result from the enquiries of a greater number of people, the moment of discovery was wholly individual. Intellectual creativity and insight could not benefit from collective enterprises. If, for Priestley, scientific practice demonstrated the limits of a 'common' pursuit of the good, he also saw in a crude version of empiricism a model for policy-makers. 'We are so little capable of arguing *a priori* in matters of government, that it should seem, experiments only can determine how far this power of the legislature ought to extend.' Until a 'sufficient number of experiments' were made the civil government was best advised to limit its 'interference' to things 'that do not immediately affect the lives, liberty, or property of the members of the community' (*Essay*, pp. 31–2). The stress put on the communal, security-oriented definition of the common good by the contemporary debates on empire and toleration is clearly reflected in the paragraphs added to the second edition of the *Essay* in 1771.

Priestley's own attempt to describe the proper balance between sovereign and subject draws on the intellectual traditions of an English dissenting enlightenment which was distinguished by the theological context of its commitment to freedom of thought. In the divisive climate of the later 1760s and early 1770s the parallels between the imperial and toleration debates renewed accusations that dissenters were disloyal. As a result, they were at pains to emphasize their fealty to Crown and country. Priestley was an especially strong exponent of the view that dissenters were enemies of tyranny precisely because of their religious status. 'And it appears to us, that the man will oppose them both with equal firmness, who is as tenacious of his religious as he is of his civil liberty' (*A View of the Principles and Conduct of the Protestant Dissenters*, in *Works*, XXII, p. 367). Priestley warned dissenters that their 'peculiar privileges and the general liberties of this country' were connected; an attack on the latter would be a threat to the former. In more provocative language he suggested that 'whenever the altar of civil tyranny shall be erected, you will be the first victims' (*An Address . . . to Dissenters*, in *Works*, XXII, p. 485).

As Martin Fitzpatrick and others have explained, the 'rational' dissent to which Priestley subscribed at this time was upheld by two principles: the centrality of scripture and the sufficiency of human reason. The assertion of a right to 'private judgement' was the expression of this Protestant ideology, and its centrality in the dissenters' programme reflects their conscious effort to describe their demands as the fulfilment of the Reformation. While it was precisely the possibility of anarchism attendant upon 'uncontrolled' exegesis that frightened non-dissenters, Priestley's response was to stress the common ground between the processes of improvement in the sciences and in religion. The accomplishments of Copernicus and Galileo on the one hand, and those of the early Protestant reformers on the other, were often cited as examples of the possible achievements of free enquiry. Why, dissenters asked, was continuing improvement in religion now to be foreclosed? Responding to William Blackstone's declaration in his highly influential *Commentaries on the Laws of Eng-*

land that public non-conformity was a criminal act, Priestley declared that this would have suppressed England's greatest thinkers. 'They were, likewise, guilty of great arrogance, because they ought to have considered, that the prevailing opinions which they called into question, had at least a greater chance to be right than their singular notions' (*Remarks on . . . Dr Blackstone's "Commentaries"*, in *Works*, XXII, p. 324). In the *Essay* Priestley likened Blackstone's prospective suppression of the 'spirit of enterprize and innovation' to Tarquin's execution of the superior part of the population (*Essay*, p. 119). Priestley's positive view of change led him to reject the claim associated with Blackstone, but which had been put forward by Hobbes in *De Cive*, that innovation led to civil war.

Just as the 'inefficiency' of government intervention created space for intellectual liberty, the inability of ecclesiastical establishments to promote the private, rational investigation of scripture delineated the limits of their coercive power. Truth was the natural object of human reason and the basis of all religious belief. It could not be displaced by the prudential considerations that figured so heavily in the powerful argument of William Warburton, *The Alliance of Church and State* (1736). Because religion was worthless if untrue, its civil establishment could only be defended because it served the cause of truth. Its 'utility' in preserving the authority of bishops and kings was necessarily subordinate to the processes of intellectual enquiry that alone brought individuals to deeper understanding. Priestley cautioned that the determinations of 'Mere Statesmen', based on 'propriety (which is the same with utility)', provided an inadequate justification for government interference in spirituals.

Priestley's repeated insistence on the 'most perfect freedom of inquiry and debate' reflects his belief that truth was the basic measure of affairs and was capable of being discerned only after a freely conducted investigation (*A Letter of Advice to Protestant Dissenters*, in *Works*, XXII, p. 455; *Essay*, p. 82). Priestley substituted this unrestricted freedom of enquiry for the more usual discussion of reforming constitutional forms, suggesting that complete freedom of thought would engender a political community in which there would no longer be a need for the solutions offered by the examples of antiquity. In Priestley's vision of politics, where information was free, so were citizens. The abandonment of any commitment to the necessity of preserving a particular form of government is yet another indication of Priestley's movement away from the traditional opposition reliance on 'ancient' politics.

While Priestley believed and hoped that free enquiry would be a means to social peace and would speed the approach towards a fully reformed Christianity, he was prepared to face the consequences of a society in which freely enquiring individuals put all beliefs and all conventions to the test.

> But should free inquiry lead to the destruction of Christianity itself, it ought not, on that account, to be discontinued; for we can only wish for the prevalence of Christianity on the supposition of its being true; and if it fall before the influence of free inquiry, it can only do so in consequence of its not being true.
> (*The Importance and Extent of Free Inquiry in Matters of Religion: A Sermon*, in *Works*, XV, p. 78)

This same readiness to countenance the destruction of fundamental social organizations such as religion and the state was also professed by Price and Cartwright, each of whom was to declare that if the British Empire could not be held together by justice it were better dissolved.

Like nearly all his contemporaries, Priestley believed that political society rested on a consensual basis: obligation was exchanged for protection. In this equation, he denied that individuals ever relinquished their 'natural right' to self-defence. However, where others, like Price, supposed a participatory regime to be the only certain means of ensuring continued security, Priestley's fundamental lack of interest in active political life is reflected in the more limited scope of his desired liberty. Priestley's focus was on individuals, and his aim was to limit the extent of government and keep it as far removed from quotidian life as possible. In the *Observations on Civil Liberty* Price had given a fourfold definition of liberty which was inspired by Samuel Clarke's insistence on a natural liberty that was modelled and described in terms of God's. Physical 'self-determination' and political 'self-government' were characteristics of all human beings. Price and Cartwright were clear proponents of 'natural equality', contending that all social distinctions were consensual. The defence of equality and self-government was taken by critics as evidence of a 'levelling' republicanism.

Priestley's 'political' liberty (the equivalent of Price's 'civil' liberty), on the contrary, described no fundamental human characteristic but was simply 'the right of magistracy', or the capacity of an individual to sit in judgement of other men or act on their behalf. 'Civil' liberty, in Priestley's view far more essential, described the horizon of an individual within which 'he has to be exempt from the control of the society, or its agents' (*Essay*, p. 12). Like Grotius but unlike Price, Priestley recognized that one could possess civil liberty – control over one's own conduct and thoughts – without any role in the management of the political community. From Priestley's point of view, political liberty was valuable simply as 'the only sure guard of civil liberty', and therefore the extent to which 'persons in common ranks of life' could partake of political liberty was an insignificant issue (*Lectures on History and General Policy*, London, 1788, p. 237; *Essay*, p. 32). Though only representative democracy could ensure that determinations of the common good reflected the actual good of individuals, Priestley denied that every individual was entitled to cast a vote for these representatives (*Present State*, p. 134). Such voting as obtained was to be based on wealth. The wealthy could cast votes for the higher offices while the poor, whose dependence made their judgement suspect, were only to vote for the lower ones (*Essay*, pp. 15–17).

Sensitive contemporaries noticed this basic difference between Price and Priestley. One little-known pamphleteer, writing in opposition to Price's defence of natural equality in the *Observations*, declared that 'I can by no means agree with this sentiment, and think rather with Doctor PRIESTLEY, "that such a pure democracy is not only not possible . . . " ' but was unlikely to benefit the majority of persons (Henry Goodricke, *Observations on Dr Price's Theory*, London, 1776, p. 99). Because civil liberty was universally proclaimed as the pre-eminent virtue of the English constitution, it was possible, with some wilful ignorance, to see Priestley's discussion as consistent with the commonplace definition. Equality and political participation, however, as proposed by Price, remained unassimilable for the vast majority of writers on politics in the eighteenth century.

Priestley's political thought is frequently linked to that of John Locke. His is a supposedly 'Lockean liberalism', and the *Essay on First Principles of Government* a 'gloss' on the *Second Treatise*. But is this correct? That same preface in which Priestley acknowledged Brown's stimulus in the genesis of the *Essay* also declared a departure from Locke's account of 'morals and policy'. And in *A Letter of Advice to Protestant Dissenters* (1774), Priestley spelled out his disagreement with Locke's position on individual rights. He admitted to having expected the hail of abuse that was generated by his writings, since he had 'advanced some new arguments, and of considerable strength, in favour of religious liberty, all preceding writers having, as far as I know, acquiesced in the argument and limits of Mr Locke . . . ' (in *Works*, XXII, p. 458).

The basis of Priestley's difficulty with Locke was the seeming ease with which Locke's defence of toleration could be employed to justify the enforcement of religious uniformity. Priestley's sensitivity to the overriding force of arguments from national security may have prompted this suspicion of Locke. In fact, many of those who supported the government position on colonial taxation and the maintenance of a religious establishment on precisely these grounds did invoke the authority of Locke to uphold the sovereignty of Parliament. Hence, because Locke's distinction between civil and spiritual spheres could be blurred by those who correctly maintained that religion was a legitimate concern of the civil ruler, Priestley sought a criterion 'of a more general and less exceptionable nature, than Mr Locke's . . . ' Instead of following Locke's division, Priestley suggested that goals best secured by 'numbers' marked off the sphere of civil authority while those best secured by individuals constituted the arena of civil liberty.

Perhaps the clearest indication of Priestley's understanding of Locke's theory of toleration is his claim that John Brown's strongly communal determination of the good actually depended on Locke's arguments. Thus, while 'certainly admirable' for the late seventeenth century, the intervening period left Locke's writings decidedly dated. Priestley singled out, in particular, the fact that 'Mr Locke was staggered at the thought of tolerating Atheism'. Priestley drew from this the conclusion that 'he might have hesitated to tolerate other opinions' now no longer believed dangerous. Hence the allegation that Brown had 'availed himself of Mr Locke's authority for intolerance' (*Letter of Advice*, in *Works*, XXII, p. 478). In the *Essay*, Priestley claimed that 'in the few particulars which Dr Brown has thought proper to mention, his intolerant principles are countenanced by Mr Locke' (*Essay*, pp. 59–60). Priestley's assertion that he had set

Introduction

forth 'a more accurate and extensive system of morals and policy, than was adopted by Mr Locke' (*Essay*, p. 3) reflects his belief that Locke remained committed to the priorities of statecraft and the ineluctably civil character of religion. On this crucial point Priestley cannot be said to be 'glossing' Locke but, rather, striking off in a new direction.

Priestley believed that he was defending a notion of freedom of thought broader than that offered by any predecessor, including Locke. From what he termed the 'Newtonian system' (*Essay*, p. 49), the generalized writings of Clarke which, as we have seen, he still endorsed in the early 1770s, came the metaphysical view of human nature based on the free exercise of reason and supported by the notion of a natural right. In practical terms, the limit of this natural right was marked by the point beyond which the community could better promote the interests of individuals. Religion, on this account, despite being a matter in which the civil magistrate could be concerned, was nevertheless beyond his ken. Let us end, then, with a speculative question. Can Priestley's politics be called 'liberal'?

He believed in the broadest possible freedom of enquiry and his notion of toleration followed from this. In terms of practical politics, Priestley's 'perfect freedom of debate' might seem unwieldy. Yet it was another contemporary, Immanuel Kant, who made freedom of information the cornerstone of the politics of civil society. Also, while fellow campaigners for toleration such as the latitudinarian Archdeacon Blackburne and the dissenters Andrew Kippis and Theophilus Lindsey were distinctly queasy about a 'universal toleration' that comprehended Roman Catholics, Priestley remained a steady and outspoken proponent of universal toleration.

Nevertheless, and this surely gives pause, the many paths of enquiry did not constitute ends in themselves. Rather, diverse modes of enquiry simply increased the probability that truth would eventually be discovered (*A View of the Principles and Conduct of the Protestant Dissenters*, in *Works*, XXII, p. 374). Hence, to choose one example, while both Priestley and later liberals can be seen to embrace the view of human nature that lies behind John Stuart Mill's 'principle of individuality', for Priestley intellectual self-fashioning remained only a means to the end of discovering truth. The powerful force of private judgement and its implications led him to endorse both pluralistic enquiry and, at the same time, the notion of ultimate convergence on a single truth. In Priestley's subsequent philosophical and theological writings the implications of this paradox drew him into wider and deeper discussions of prophecy and messianism. In the 1760s and 1770s, however, this contradiction was only beginning to become apparent. In the meantime he appeared to his contemporaries as the philosopher and intellectual enquirer *par excellence*, to whom Jefferson declared that 'yours is one of the few lives precious to mankind of which every thinking man is solicitous'.

Chronology of Joseph Priestley's life

1733   Born 13 March
1745–9 Batley Grammar School
1751   Daventry Academy
1755   Minister at Needham Market, Suffolk
1758   Minister at Nantwich, Cheshire
1761   Appointed tutor in languages and belles-lettres at Warrington Academy; *The Rudiments of an English Grammar*
1762   *A Course of Lectures on the Theory of Language*
1765   *An Essay on a Course of Liberal Education*
1767   Minister at Mill Hill Chapel, Leeds; *The History and Present State of Electricity*
1768   *Essay on the First Principles of Government* (1st edn); *A Free Address to Protestant Dissenters* (1st edn)
1769   *Considerations on Church Authority; A View of the Principles and Conduct of the Protestant Dissenters; The Present State Of Liberty in Great Britain and her Colonies; Remarks on . . . Dr Blackstone's "Commentaries"*
1770   Founded Leeds Circulating Library; *A Familiar Introduction to the Theory and Practice of Perspective*
1771   Offered appointment as official astronomer to James Cook's second expedition; *Essay on First Principles of Government* (2nd edn); *A Free Address to Protestant Dissenters* (2nd edn)
1772   Appointed librarian and 'literary companion' to the Earl of Shelburne, on Richard Price's recommendation; *Institutes of Natural and Revealed Religion* (Vol. I; Vol. II in 1773 and Vol. III in 1774); *The History of the Present State of Discoveries Relating to Vision, Light and Colours*

1774   Discovery of dephlogisticated air; *Experiments and Observations on Different Kinds of Air* (6 vols., 1774–86); *An Address to . . . Dissenters . . . on the Approaching Election*; *A Letter of Advice to Protestant Dissenters*; *An Examination of . . . Reid . . . Beattie . . . and Oswald*

1775   *Hartley's Theory of the Human Mind*

1777   *Disquisitions Relating to Matter and Spirit*

1778   *A Free Discussion of . . . Materialism and Philosophical Necessity . . . between Dr Price and Dr Priestley*

1780   Separation from Shelburne; moved to Birmingham and elected minister of the New Meeting; *A Free Address . . . in Favour of the Roman Catholics*; *Letters to a Philosophical Unbeliever*

1782   *An History of the Corruptions of Christianity*

1787   *An Address to the Subscribers to the Birmingham Library, on the . . . Motion to Restrict . . . the Choice of Books*; *Account of a Society for the Relief of the Industrious Poor*

1788   *Lectures on History and General Policy* (delivered at Warrington 1761–7)

1791   January: vindicated French Revolution in *Letters to Burke*: *A Political Dialogue on the General Principles of Government*
       14 July: mob attacked and destroyed his house, laboratory and church
       November: elected to replace his recently deceased friend Richard Price as preacher at the Gravel Pit, Hackney

1793   His sons emigrate to the United States of America; *Letters to the Philosophers and Politicians of France . . . on Religion*

1794   7 April: Priestley emigrates with his wife to the United States
       11 July: Priestley moves to Northumberland, Pennsylvania
       November: Declined chair in chemistry in Philadelphia; *Discourses on the Evidences of Revealed Religion*

1796   17 September: Wife dies; *Considerations on the Doctrine of Phlogiston and the Decomposition of Air*

1804   Priestley dies 6 February

Biographical guide

PETER ANNET (1693–1769) was a deist whose attack on the veracity of biblical history led to a conviction for blasphemy in 1763.

THOMAS BALGUY (1716–85), a Fellow of St John's College, Cambridge, and lecturer on moral philosophy. His father (John Balguy) was a noted latitudinarian and it was his connection with the latitudinarian bishop Benjamin Hoadly that secured preferment for his son; nevertheless Thomas opposed the abolition of subscription. A friend of William Warburton, he was offered the vacant see of Gloucester after Warburton's death in 1771.

FRANCIS BLACKBURNE (1705–87) was a contemporary of Edmund Law and John Brown at Cambridge. His attack on W. S. Powell's defence of subscription ultimately led to the publication of the *Confessional*, the founding document of the later eighteenth-century demand for a wider, legally established religious toleration. His sons-in-law were John Disney and Theophilus Lindsey, friends of Richard Price and Joseph Priestley and themselves important non-conformists.

WILLIAM BLACKSTONE (1728–80) was Vinerian Professor of Law at Oxford and later a Member of Parliament. His lectures were published as the *Commentaries on the Laws of England*, the instantly definitive early modern analysis of English law. Blackstone grounded the common law on the principles of the modern natural law theory, producing a powerful defence of the power of the state. It was precisely Blackstone's readiness to condemn religious heterodoxy that drew him into polemical confrontation with Priestley in 1769.

EDMUND BONNER (1500–69), Bishop of London. Like Stephen Gardiner, Bonner resisted Somerset's attempt to bring church governance under the control of Privy Council. Also like Gardiner, he was liberated from prison by Mary Tudor and took an active role in the famous persecutions of Protestants that followed.

JOHN BROWN (1715–66) was an undergraduate at Cambridge and subsequently went to Carlisle as a minor canon. He gained support through Warburton and wrote broadly on culture and politics, becoming famous as 'Estimate' Brown for a dismal, though very popular, assessment of Britain's future during the Seven Years War.

JAMES BURGH (1714–75) was schoolmaster of the dissenting academy at Stoke Newington and famous for *Political Disquisitions* (3 vols., 1774–5); it was constantly cited by contemporaries as a mine of information on the causes and remedies of corruption. The book is a compendium of citations from English opposition thinkers of the seventeenth and eighteenth centuries showing how the 'Good Old Cause' was successfully, and unsuccessfully, adapted to the contemporary problems of the empire and the state.

JOHN CARTWRIGHT (1740–1824) was a prosperous naval officer, manufacturer and inventor who refused to take up his commission against the American rebels. He began his career with pamphlets attacking the British position in the colonial dispute but then turned his attention to abuses at home, founded the *Society for Constitutional Information* and led the movement for parliamentary reform.

SAMUEL CLARKE (1675–1729) was confidant of Newton and Queen Caroline, Boyle Lecturer 1704–5 and minister of St James's Westminster. Clark was attacked as an Arian by fellow churchmen. He articulated a philosophy of natural religion that failed to convince sceptics and terrified dogmatists but which nourished two successive generations of non-conformist thinkers.

STEPHEN GARDINER (1483–1555), diplomat and Bishop of

Winchester, who served Henry VIII on several Continental embassies. As a strong defender of episcopacy, his loyalty was suspected by Henry and his resistance to change led to his imprisonment. After the accession of Mary he was freed and became notorious for his role in the subsequent persecutions.

EDMUND GIBSON (1669–1748) was Bishop of London and wrote extensively on church polity. He attacked Francis Atterbury's proposal to increase the powers of the Lower House of Convocation and defenders of Samuel Clarke, such as John Jackson, for what he perceived to be their defence of free thought and deism.

DAVID HARTLEY (1705–57) was a medical doctor whose career had been launched by his refusal to subscribe to the Thirty-Nine Articles at Cambridge. He is best remembered for his *Observations on Man* and the thoroughness with which he expounded the theory of association suggested by Locke and John Gay.

BENJAMIN HOADLY (1676–1761), successively Bishop of Bangor, Hereford, Winchester and Salisbury, and a leading figure in both religious and political polemic. High churchmen attacked his hostility to religious establishments as a manifestation of the levelling republicanism which they perceived in his contractualist and Ciceronian defence of the Revolution of 1688. These remain pronounced in his less well-known letters as *Britannicus* for the Walpolian *London Journal* which show how Revolution Principles and the needs of the state were consistent.

FRANCES HUTCHESON (1694–1746) was an Irish thinker who held the chair in moral philosophy at Glasgow, where he published extensively and taught a generation of leading thinkers. His references to both a 'moral sense' and the pre-emptive force of pleasure and pain made interpretation a battlefield for rival contemporary schools eager to claim him for their ranks.

ANDREW KIPPIS (1725–95) was a Presbyterian minister, teacher at Hackney academy, regular contributor to *Monthly Review*, editor of the second edition of the *Biographia Britannica* and stalwart proponent of wide toleration.

JOHN KNOX (1505–72) Scottish ecclesiastical reformer and author of important tracts justifying resistance to Mary Tudor (e.g. *First Blast of the Trumpet against the Monstrous Regiment of Women*). These remain basic texts for the study of sixteenth-century resistance theory.

THEOPHILUS LINDSEY (1723–1808) was the son-in-law of Francis Blackburne and friend of Priestley. When the Feathers Tavern Petition to end subscription failed in 1772 he withdrew from the church and established the Essex Street Unitarian Chapel.

RICHARD PRICE (1723–91), Arian minister, moral philosopher and actuary who wrote on the public debt, public morals and empire. An intimate friend of Franklin and Priestley and correspondent of Turgot, he became notorious and was widely hated for his defence of the American Revolution and the early stages of the French.

GRANVILLE SHARP (1735–1813), a Greek and Hebrew scholar and the leading abolitionist in late-eighteenth-century Britain, largely responsible for the abolition of slavery in Britain in 1772. He wrote *A Defence of the People's Natural Right to a Share in the Legislature* and resigned his job in the Ordnance Department so as not to contribute to the war effort.

WILLIAM WARBURTON (1698–1779) was Bishop of Gloucester and friend of poets, writers and aristocrats. He was chaplain to Frederick Prince of Wales and theorist of the symbiotic relationship between civil and religious establishments. His *Alliance between Church and State* spelled out the purely political role of a religious establishment in terms so clear as to make both high churchmen and nonconformists disagree, though for different reasons.

JOHN WILKES (1727–97), while a friend and correspondent of leading European thinkers, is best known as the provocative popular politician of the 1769s. His career as the focus for political discontent began with the attempt to suppress his publication of No. 45 of the *North Briton* and culminated with the thrice-disputed Middlesex election to the House of Commons in 1768.

Bibliographical guide

English Radicalism

The basic study of opposition political thought in eighteenth-century Britain is Caroline Robbins' *The Eighteenth-Century Commonwealthman* (Cambridge, MA, 1959) and her collection of essays, *Absolute Liberty: A Selection from the Articles and Papers of Caroline Robbins*, ed. Barbara Taft (Hamden, CT, 1982). John Brewer, *Party Ideology and Popular Politics at the Accession of George III* (Cambridge, 1976) and Ian R. Christie, *Wilkes, Wyvill and Reform* (London, 1962) remain valuable discussions of politics both within Parliament and without in the crucial third quarter of the eighteenth century. Colin Bonwick's *English Radicals and the American Revolution* (Chapel Hill, NC, 1977) is a fine discussion of the relationship between the imperial crisis and the Radicals. Isaac Kramnick's *Republicanism and Bourgeois Radicalism* (Ithaca, 1990) and J. C. D. Clark's *English Society 1688–1832* (Cambridge, 1985) offer dramatically divergent assessments of the nature and contribution of 'radical' political thought. Only Richard Price has found a biographer worthy of the subject (D. O. Thomas, *The Honest Mind: The Thought and Work of Richard Price*, (Oxford, 1977). James Burgh has been ably discussed by Carla Hay, in *James Burgh, Spokesman for Reform in Hanoverian England* (Washington, DC, 1979), but for understanding the philosophical foundation of his political thought, Martha Kaderly Zebrowsky's *One Cato is not Enough; or, how James Burgh found nature's duty and real authority and secured the dignity of human nature against all manner of public abuse, iniquitous practice, corruption, vice, and irreligion* (unpublished PhD, Columbia University,

1982) is essential. John Osborne's *John Cartwright* (Cambridge, 1972) is fundamentally flawed for having made no reference to the earlier work of Naomi H. Churgin (Miller) ('John Cartwright and Radical Parliamentary Reform, 1808–1819', *English Historical Review* 83 (1968), pp. 705–28; *Major John Cartwright: A Study in Radical Parliamentary Reform, 1774–1824*, unpublished PhD, Columbia University, 1963). For a detailed account of Cartwright's role as catalyst as well as theorist, see David Drinkwater-Lunn, *John Cartwright, Political Education and English Radicalism 1774–1794* (unpublished DPhil, Oxford, 1970).

Priestley's life and background

Not surprisingly, each of Priestley's recent biographers has denounced the incomplete efforts of their predecessors. Unfortunately, and perhaps inevitably, the complete Priestley has not yet been described. The best short account remains that of Rev. Alexander Gordon and Sir Philip J. Hartog in Volume 46 of the *Dictionary of National Biography*. Other descriptions of his life are given by Thomas Edward Thorpe, *Joseph Priestley* (London, 1906); Anne Durning Holt, *A Life of Joseph Priestley* (London, 1931); and Frederick William Gibbs, *Joseph Priestley, Adventurer in Science and Champion of Truth* (London, 1965). Robert E. Schofield has culled from Priestley's letters and papers *A Scientific Autobiography of Joseph Priestley 1733–1804* (Cambridge, MA, 1966) with commentary. The basic source for all biographers remains the *Memoirs of Joseph Priestley, Written by Himself*, first published in 1804 and reprinted many times subsequently. But note that the letters included by J. T. Rutt in Volume I of his edition of the *Collected Works* (London 1817–31, 25 vols.) are extremely selective.

Priestley and dissent

The history of later-eighteenth-century rational dissent remains largely dependent on older studies: Anthony Lincoln, *Some Political and Social Ideas of English Dissent 1763–1800* (Cambridge, 1938); Richard Burgess Barlow, *Citizenship and Conscience* (Philadelphia, 1962); and Gerald R. Cragg, *Reason and Authority in the Eighteenth Century* (Cambridge, 1964). Martin Fitzpatrick has written several

incisive and important articles about Priestley, including 'Joseph
Priestley and the Cause of Universal Toleration', *The Price-Priestley
Newsletter*, 1 (1977), pp.3–30; and 'Joseph Priestley and the Millen-
nium', in *Science, Medicine and Dissent: Joseph Priestley (1733–1804)*,
eds. R. G. W. Anderson and Christopher Lawrence, London, 1987,
pp. 29–38. James E. Bradley, in his most recent book, *Religion,
Revolution and English Radicalism: Non-conformity in Eighteenth-Century Politics and Society* (Cambridge, 1990), argues that the role of
Priestley, Price and their friends in the politics of toleration has been
overstated. The crucial and complicated issue of the relationship
between rational dissenting theology (especially Priestley's) and
politics has been plumbed in several important articles: J. G. McEvoy
and J. E. McGuire, 'God and Nature: Priestley's Way of Rational
Dissent', *Historical Studies in the Physical Sciences*, 6 (1975), pp. 325–
404; Mark Philp, 'Rational Religion and Political Radicalism',
Enlightenment and Dissent, 4 (1985), pp. 35–46; and Martin
Fitzpatrick, 'Heretical Religion and Radical Political Ideas in Late
Eighteenth-Century England', in *The Transformation of Political
Culture: England and Germany in the Late Eighteenth Century*, ed. Eck-
hart Hellmuth (Oxford, 1990), pp. 339–74.

Priestley and science

Martin Fitzpatrick's review article, 'Science and Society in the
Enlightenment', *Enlightenment and Dissent*, 4 (1985), pp. 83–106, is a
useful starting point. Robert E. Schofield, 'Joseph Priestley:
Theology, Physics and Metaphysics', *Enlightenment and Dissent*, 2
(1983), pp. 69–82, has attempted to place these different intellectual
disciplines in some relationship. J. G. McEvoy has concentrated on
delineating the metaphysical principles behind Priestley's experimen-
tal science: 'Joseph Priestley, "Aerial Philosopher": Metaphysics and
Methodology in Priestley's Chemical Thought, from 1772 to 1781',
Ambix, 25 (1978), pp. 1–55, 93–116, 153–75; 'Enlightenment and
Dissent in Science: Joseph Priestley and the Limits of Theoretical
Reasoning', *Enlightenment and Dissent*, 2 (1983), pp. 47–68; and
'Causes and Laws, Powers and Principles: The Metaphysical
Foundations of Priestley's Concept of Phlogiston', in *Science, Medicine
and Dissent: Joseph Priestley (1733–1804)*, eds. R. G. W. Anderson and
Christopher Lawrence (London, 1987), pp. 55–72. Simon Schaffer

has placed Priestley into the context of eighteenth-century natural philosophy that he has been developing: 'Priestley's Questions: An Historiographic Survey', *History of Science*, 22 (1984), pp. 151–83; 'Priestley and the Politics of Spirit', in *Science, Medicine and Dissent: Joseph Priestley (1733–1804)*, eds. R. G. W. Anderson and Christopher Lawrence (London, 1987), pp. 39–54. For Priestley's relationship with Antoine Lavoisier, see Aaron J. Ihde's 'Priestley and Lavoisier', in *Joseph Priestley: Scientist, Theologian and Metaphysician*, eds. Lester Kieft and Bennet R. Willeford, Jr (Lewisburg and London, 1980), pp. 62–91. Maurice Crossland has argued the political implications of Priestley's science in 'The Image of Science as a Threat: Burke versus Priestley and the "Philosophic Revolution"', *British Journal for the History of Science*, 20 (1987), pp. 277–308.

Priestley's politics

The best introduction is D. O. Thomas, 'Progress, Liberty and Utility: The Political Philosophy of Joseph Priestley', in *Science, Medicine and Dissent: Joseph Priestley (1733–1804)*, eds. R. G. W. Anderson and Christopher Lawrence (London, 1987), pp. 73–80. Margaret Canovan, 'Two Concepts of Liberty – Eighteenth Century Style', *The Price-Priestley Newsletter*, 2 (1978), pp. 27–43, is a very valuable discussion of the concept of liberty as used by Priestley. Jack Fruchtman, Jr's *The Apocalyptic Politics of Richard Price and Joseph Priestley*, in *Transactions of the American Philosophical Society* (Philadelphia, 1983), is marred by insensitivity to the divergent intellectual contexts in which the thought of both Price and Priestley must be located. Jenny Graham's survey of Priestley's political life offers an alternative: 'Revolutionary Philosopher: The Political Ideas of Joseph Priestley (1733–1804) Part One', *Enlightenment and Dissent*, 8 (1989), pp. 43–68; and 'Part Two', 9 (1990) pp. 14–46. Margaret Canovan, 'Priestley on Rank', *Enlightenment and Dissent*, 2 (1983), pp. 27–32, and Ruth Watts, 'Joseph Priestley and Education', *Enlightenment and Dissent*, 2 (1983), pp. 83–100, are important discussions of seeming paradoxes in Priestley's political thought.

A note on the text

The text used for the *Essay on the First Principles of Government* is based on the second, 'corrected and enlarged' edition, printed for J. Johnson in 1771. Square brackets [] indicate material that was added to this edition and which did not appear in the first edition (1768). Because Sections VI, VII and IX were wholly new additions brackets have not been used.

The asterisked footnotes are Priestley's; the rest are my own. The original footnotes providing page references for the quotations from Warburton's *Alliance* have been deleted because I have not been able to trace the edition used by Priestley.

A N

E S S A Y

ON THE

FIRST PRINCIPLES

O F

GOVERNMENT,

AND ON THE NATURE OF

Political, Civil, and Religious

LIBERTY,

INCLUDING

Remarks on Dr. BROWN's *Code of Education,*

AND ON

DR. BALGUY's Sermon on CHURCH AUTHORITY.

The SECOND EDITION, corrected and enlarged,

By JOSEPH PRIESTLEY, LL.D.F.R.S.

L O N D O N:

Printed for J. JOHNSON, No. 72, in St. Paul's Church-Yard.
MDCCLXXI.

The Contents.

SECTION I.—*Of the first principles of government,
and the different kinds of liberty*   p. 8
II.   *Of political liberty*   13
III.   *Of civil liberty*   28
IV.   *In what manner an authoritative code of education would
affect political and civil liberty*   39
V.   *Of religious liberty, and toleration in general*   52
VI.   *Some distinctions that have been made on the subject
of religious liberty, and toleration considered*   63
VII.   *Farther observations concerning the extent of
ecclesiastical authority, and the power of civil governors in
matters of religion*   69
VIII. *Of the necessity, or utility, of ecclesiastical establishments*   81
IX.   *A review of some particular positions of Dr Balguy's on
the subject of church-authority*   91
X.   *Of the progress of civil societies to a state of greater
perfection, showing that it is retarded by encroachments
on civil and religious liberty*   107

The Preface.

This publication owes its rise to the *Remarks* I wrote on *Dr Brown's proposal for a code of education*. Several persons who were pleased to think favourably of that performance, (in which I was led to mention the subject of civil and religious liberty) were desirous that I should treat of it more at large, and without any immediate view to the Doctor's work. It appeared to them, that some of the views I had given of this important, but difficult subject, were new, and showed it, in a clearer light than any in which they had seen it represented before; and they thought I had placed the foundation of some of the most valuable interests of mankind on a broader and firmer basis[1], than Mr Locke, and others who had formerly written upon this subject. I have endeavoured to answer the wishes of my friends, in the best manner I am able; and, at the same time, I have retained the substance of the former treatise, having distributed the several parts of it into the body of this.

In this *second edition*, I have also introduced what I had written on *Church-authority*, in answer to *Dr Balguy's* sermon on that subject, preached at Lambeth chapel, and published by order of the Archbishop. As I do not mean to republish either the *Remarks on Dr Brown*, or these on *Dr Balguy*, separately, and the subjects of both those pieces have a near relation to the general one on *Civil and Religious Liberty*, I thought there would be a propriety in throwing them into one treatise.

[1] In the first edition this was followed by ' . . . in consequence of my availing myself of a more accurate and extensive system of morals and policy, than was adopted by Mr Locke, and others . . . '

I had no thoughts of animadverting upon Dr Warburton in this work, till I was informed by some intelligent and worthy clergymen of my acquaintance, that his *Alliance* is generally considered as the best defence of the present system of church-authority, and that most other writers took their arguments from it.

In a postscript to this work he informs us, p. 271, that, in it, *the reader will see confuted at large*, what he calls *a puritanical principle*, and also *an absurd assertion of Hooker's, by which he entangled himself and his cause in inextricable difficulties*, viz. *that civil and ecclesiastical power are things separated by nature, and more especially by divine institution; and so independent of one another, that they must always continue independent.* Whatever success this writer may have had in pulling up other foundations, I think he had better have left those of the church as he found them: for the difficulties in which the scheme of the *Alliance* is entangled, appear to me to be far more inextricable, than those of any other scheme of church-authority that I have yet seen. All that can be said in its favour is, that, having less of the simplicity of truth, and, consequently, being supported with more art and sophistry, the absurdity of it is not so obvious at first sight, though it be ten times more glaring after it has been sufficiently attended to.

Sorry I am to be under the necessity of troubling my reader with the repetition of any thing that has been said before on this subject, in my remarks on those writers; but when the same arguments are urged again and again, it is impossible always to find new, or better answers. I flatter myself, however, that several of the observations in this treatise will appear to be new, at least, that some things will appear to be set in a new or clearer point of light. But whenever the interests of truth and liberty are attacked, it is to be wished that some would stand up in their defence, whether they acquit themselves better than their predecessors in the same *good old cause*, or not. *New books* in defence of any principles whatever, will be read by many persons, who will not look into *old books*, for the proper answers to them.

Considerable advantage cannot but accrue to the cause of religious, as well as civil liberty, from keeping the important subject continually in view. We are under great obligation, therefore, to all the advocates for church-authority, whenever they are pleased to write in its defence.

Every attempt that has hitherto been made to shake, or undermine the foundations of the christian faith, hath ended in the firmer establishment of it. Also, every attempt to support the unjust claims of churchmen over their fellow christians, hath been equally impotent, and hath recoiled upon themselves; and, I make no doubt, that this will be the issue of all the future efforts of interested or misguided men, in so weak and unworthy a cause.

It will be seen, that I have taken no notice of any thing that has been written in the controversy about the *Confessional*. I would only observe, and I cannot help observing, that the violent opposition that has been made to the modest attempts, both of the *candid disquisitors*, and those of the author of the *Confessional*, and his respectable friends, to procure a redress of only a few of the more intolerable grievances the clergy labour under, and a removal of some of the most obvious and capital defects in the established church, has more weight than a hundred arguments drawn from *theory* only, in demonstrating the folly of erecting such complicated and unwieldy systems of policy, and in showing the mischiefs that attend them.

Little did the founders of church establishments consider, of what unspeakable importance it is to the interests of religion, that the ambition of christian ministers be circumscribed within narrow limits, when they left them such unbounded scope for courting preferment. But the interests of religion have been very little considered by the founders of church establishments. Indeed if they had considered them, how little were they qualified to make provision for them? I need not say what I feel, when I find so much in the writings of ingenious men concerning *the wisdom* of these constitutions. It always brings to my mind what St Paul says of *the wisdom of this world* in other respects.

Such, however, is the virtue of some men, that it is proof against all the bad influence of the constitution of which they are members. Without flattering, or tormenting themselves with a *vain ambition*, many excellent clergymen, worthy of a better situation, contentedly sit down to the proper duty of their station. Their only object is *to do good to the souls of men*, and their only hope of reward is in that world, where *they who have been wise shall shine as the brightness of the firmament, and they who have turned many to righteousness as the stars for ever and ever.* Such characters as these I truly revere; and it is chiefly for the sake of forming more such, that I wish the establishment of the church of England might be reformed in some essential points. The powers of reason and conscience plead for such a reformation, but, alas! the

5

powers of this world are against it. This unnatural *ally* of religion (or rather her imperious *master*) without whose permission nothing can be done, will not admit of it.

But at the same time that, from a love of truth, and a just regard for the purity of a divine religion, we bear a public testimony against those abuses which men have introduced into it; let us, as becomes christians, have the candour to make proper allowances for the prejudices and prepossessions, even of the founders, promoters, and abettors of these anti-christian systems; and still farther let us be from indulging a thought to the prejudice of those, who have been educated in a reverence for these modes of religion, and have not strength of mind to separate their ideas of these *forms*, from those of the *power* of it. In this case, let us be particularly careful how we give offence to any serious and well-disposed minds, and patiently bear with the wheat and the tares growing together till the harvest.

Such is my belief in the doctrine of an over-ruling providence, that I have no doubt, but that every thing in the whole system of nature, how noxious soever it may be in some respects, has real, though unknown uses; and also that every thing, even the grossest abuses in the civil or ecclesiastical constitutions of particular states, is subservient to the wise and gracious designs of him, who, notwithstanding these appearances, still *rules in the kingdoms of men*.

I make no apology for the *freedom* with which I have written. The subject is, in the highest degree, interesting to humanity, it is open to philosophical discussion, and I have taken no greater liberties than becomes a philosopher, a man, and an Englishman. Having no other views than to promote a thorough knowledge of this important subject, not being sensible of any bias to mislead me in my inquiries, and conscious of the uprightness of my intentions, I freely submit my thoughts to the examination of all impartial judges, and the friends of their country and of mankind. They who know the fervour of generous feelings will be sensible, that I have expressed myself with no more warmth than the importance of the subject necessarily prompted, in a breast not naturally the coldest; and that to have appeared more indifferent, I could not have been sincere.

Besides the freedom with which I have made this defence of civil and religious liberty, is sufficiently justified by the freedom with which they have been attacked; and though the advocates for church power are very ready to accuse the Dissenters of *indecency*, when, in defending themselves, they reflect upon the established church; yet I do not see why, in a judgment of equity, the same civility and decency should not be observed on both sides; or why insolence on one side should not be answered by contempt on the other.

Notwithstanding the ardour of mind with which, it will be evident, some parts of the following treatise were written, the warmth with which I have espoused the cause of liberty, and the severity with which I have animadverted upon whatever I apprehend to be unfavourable to it; I think I cannot be justly accused of *party zeal*, because it will be found, that I have treated all parties with equal freedom. Indeed, such is the usual violence of human passions, when any thing interesting to them is contended for, that the best cause in the world is not sufficient to prevent intemperance and excess; so that it is easy to see too much to blame in all parties: and it by no means follows, that, because a man disapproves of the conduct of one, that he must, therefore, approve of that of its opposite. The greatest enemy of popery may see something he dislikes in the conduct of the first reformers, the warmest zeal against episcopacy is consistent with the just sense of the faults of the puritans, and much more may an enemy of Charles the first, be an enemy of Cromwell also.

N. B. Let it be observed, that, in this treatise, I propose no more than to consider the *first principles* of civil and religious liberty, and to explain some leading ideas upon the subject. For a more extensive view of it, as affecting a greater variety of particulars in the system of government, I refer to *the course of lectures on history and civil policy*; a *syllabus* of which is printed in the *Essay on a course of liberal education for civil and active life*, and the whole of which, with enlargements, I propose to publish in due time.

SECTION I

Of the First Principles of Government, and the different kinds of Liberty.

Man derives two capital advantages from the superiority of his intellectual powers. The first is, that, as an individual, he possesses a certain comprehension of mind, whereby he contemplates and enjoys the past and the future, as well as the present. This comprehension is enlarged with the experience of every day; and by this means the happiness of man, as he advances in intellect, is continually less dependent on temporary circumstances and sensations.[2]

---

[2] In the first edition, this was followed by 'Ideas collected from a certain limited space, on each side of the present moment, are always ready to crowd upon his mind, and to temper, and exalt his feelings.

'This space, which is the sphere of a man's comprehension, of which he has the enjoyment, and which may be called the extent of his *present time*, is greater or less, in proportion to the progress he has made in intellect, and his advancement above mere animal nature; and it is generally growing larger during the whole course of our lives. A child is sensible of nothing beyond the present moment, being little more than a brute animal; though the actual feelings of persons advanced in life never depend wholly upon the present moment, but are greatly influenced both by the remembrance of what is past, and the expectation of what is future.

'These intellectual pleasures and pains, in many cases, wholly overpower all temporary sensations; whereby some men, of great and superior minds, enjoy a state of permanent and equable felicity, in a great measure independent of the uncertain accidents of life. In such minds the ideas of things that are seen to be the cause and effect of one another, perfectly coalesce into one, and present but one common image. Thus all the ideas of evil absolutely vanish, in the idea of the greater good with which it is connected, or of which it is productive.

'To this comprehension of mind, which is extending with the experience of every day, no bounds can be set. Nay, it should seem, that while our faculties of perception and action remain in the same vigour, our progress towards perfection must be continually accelerated; and that nothing but a future existence, in advantageous circumstances, is requisite to advance a mere man above every thing we can now conceive of excellence and perfection. This train of thought may, in some measure, enable us to conceive wherein consists the superiority of angelic beings, whose sphere of comprehension, that is, whose *present time* may be of proportionately greater extent than ours, owing to the greater extent of their recollection and foresight; and even give us some faint idea of the

The next advantage resulting from the same principle, and which is, in many respects, both the cause and effect of the former, is, that the human species itself is capable of a similar and unbounded improvement; whereby mankind in a later age are greatly superior to mankind in a former age, the individuals being taken at the same time of life. Of this progress of the species, brute animals are more incapable than they are of that relating to individuals. No horse of this age seems to have any advantage over other horses of former ages; and if there be any improvement in the species, it is owing to our manner of breeding and training them. But a man at this time, who has been tolerably well educated, in an improved christian country, is a being possessed of much greater power, to be, and to make happy, than a person of the same age, in the same, or any other country, some centuries ago. And, for this reason, I make no doubt, that a person some centuries hence will, at the same age, be as much superior to us.

The great instrument in the hand of divine providence, of this progress of the species towards perfection, is *society*, and consequently *government*. In a state of nature the powers of any individual are dissipated by an attention to a multiplicity of objects. The employments of all are similar. From generation to generation every man does the same that every other does, or has done, and no person begins where another ends; at least, general improvements are exceedingly slow, and uncertain. This we see exemplified in all barbarous nations, and especially in countries thinly inhabited, where the connections of the people are slight, and consequently society and government very imperfect; and it may be seen more particularly in North America, and Greenland. Whereas a state of more perfect society admits of a proper distribution and division of the objects of human attention. In such a state, men are connected with and subservient to one another; so that, while one man confines himself to one single object, another may give the same undivided attention to another object.

Thus the powers of all have their full effect; and hence arise

incomprehensible excellence and happiness of the Divine Being, in whose view nothing is past or future, but to whom the whole compass of duration is, to every real purpose, without distinction present.

Who fills his own eternal NOW,
And sees our ages waste.
–[Isaac] Watts'

9

improvements in all the conveniences of life, and in every branch of knowledge. In this state of things, it requires but a few years to comprehend the whole preceding progress of any one art or science; and the rest of a man's life, in which his faculties are the most perfect, may be given to the extension of it. If, by this means, one art or science should grow too large for an easy comprehension, in a moderate space of time, a commodious subdivision will be made. Thus all knowledge will be subdivided and extended; and *knowledge*, as Lord *Bacon* observes, being *power*, the human powers will, in fact, be enlarged; nature, including both its materials, and its laws, will be more at our command; men will make their situation in this world abundantly more easy and comfortable; they will probably prolong their existence in it, and will grow daily more happy, each in himself, and more able (and, I believe, more disposed) to communicate happiness to others. Thus, whatever was the beginning of this world, the end will be glorious and paradisaical, beyond what our imaginations can now conceive. Extravagant as some may suppose these views to be, I think I could show them to be fairly suggested by the true theory of human nature, and to arise from the natural course of human affairs. But, for the present, I wave this subject, the contemplation of which always makes me happy.

Government being the great instrument of this progress of the human species towards this glorious state, that form of government will have a just claim to our approbation which favours this progress, and that must be condemned in which it is retarded. Let us then, my fellow citizens, consider the business of government with these enlarged views, and trace some of the fundamental principles of it, by an attention to what is most conducive to the happiness of mankind at present, and most favourable to the increase of this happiness in futurity; and, perhaps, we may understand this intricate subject, with some of its most important circumstances, better than we have done; at least we may see some of them in a clearer and stronger point of light.

To begin with first principles, we must, for the sake of gaining clear ideas on the subject, do what almost all political writers have done before us; that is, we must suppose a number of people existing, who experience the inconvenience of living independent and unconnected; who are exposed, without redress, to insults and wrongs of every kind, and are too weak to procure themselves many of the advantages, which they are sensible might easily be compassed by united strength. These people, if they would engage the protection of the whole body, and join their force in enterprizes and undertakings calculated for their common good, must voluntarily resign some part of their natural liberty, and submit their conduct to the direction of the community: for without these concessions, such an alliance, attended with such advantages, could not be formed.

Were these people few in number, and living within a small distance of one another, it might be easy for them to assemble upon every occasion, in which the whole body was concerned; and every thing might be determined by the votes of the majority, provided they had previously agreed that the votes of a majority should be decisive. But were the society numerous, their habitations remote, and the occasions on which the whole body must interpose frequent, it would be absolutely impossible that all the members of the state should assemble, or give their attention to public business. In this case, though, with *Rousseau*[3] it be a giving up of their liberty, there must be deputies, or public officers, appointed to act in the name of the whole body; and, in a state of very great extent, where all the people could never be assembled, the whole power of the community must necessarily, and almost irreversibly, be lodged in the hands of these deputies. In England, the king, the hereditary lords, and the electors of the house of commons, are these *standing* deputies; and the members of the house of commons are, again, the *temporary* deputies of this last order of the state.

In all states, great or small, the sentiments of that body of men in whose hands the supreme power of the society is lodged, must be understood to be the sentiments of the whole body, if there be no other method in which the sentiments of the whole body can be expressed. These deputies, or representatives of the people, will make a wrong judgment, and pursue wrong measures, if they consult not the good of the whole society, whose representatives they are; just as the people themselves would make a wrong judgment, and pursue wrong measures, if they did not consult their own good, provided they could be assembled for that purpose. No maxims or rules of policy can be binding upon them, but such as they themselves shall judge to be conducive to the public good. Their own reason and conscience

---

[3] Jean-Jacques Rousseau, French music critic and philosopher.

are their only guide, and the people, in whose name they act, their only judge.

In these circumstances, if I be asked what I mean by *liberty*, I should choose, for the sake of greater clearness, to divide it into two kinds, *political* and *civil*; and the importance of having clear ideas on this subject will be my apology for the innovation. POLITICAL LIBERTY, I would say, *consists in the power, which the members of the state reserve to themselves, of arriving at the public offices, or, at least, of having votes in the nomination of those who fill them*: and I would choose to call CIVIL LIBERTY *that power over their own actions, which the members of the state reserve to themselves, and which their officers must not infringe.*

Political liberty, therefore, is equivalent to the right of magistracy, being the claim that any member of the state hath, to have his private opinion or judgment become that of the public, and thereby control the actions of others; whereas *civil liberty*, extends no farther than to a man's own conduct, and signifies the right he has to be exempt from the control of the society, or its agents; that is, the power he has of providing for his own advantage and happiness. It is a man's civil liberty, which is originally in its full force, and part of which he sacrifices when he enters into a state of society; and political liberty is that which he may, or may not acquire in the compensation he receives for it. For he may either stipulate to have a voice in the public determinations, or, as far as the public determination doth take place, he may submit to be governed wholly by others. Of these two kinds of liberty, which it is of the greatest importance to distinguish, I shall treat in the order in which I have mentioned them.

SECTION II.

Of Political Liberty.

In countries where every member of the society enjoys an equal power of arriving at the supreme offices, and consequently of directing the strength and the sentiments of the whole community, there is a state of the most perfect political liberty. On the other hand, in countries where a man is, by his birth or fortune, excluded from these offices, or from a power of voting for proper persons to fill them; that man, whatever be the form of the government, or whatever civil liberty, or power over his own actions he may have, has no power over those of another; he has no share in the government, and therefore has no political liberty at all. Nay his own conduct, as far as the society does interfere, is, in all cases, directed by others.

It may be said, that no society on earth was ever formed in the manner represented above. I answer, it is true; because all governments whatever have been, in some measure, compulsory, tyrannical, and oppressive in their origin; but the method I have described must be allowed to be the only equitable and fair method of forming a society. And since every man retains, and can never be deprived of his natural right (founded on a regard to the general good) of relieving himself from all oppression, that is, from every thing that has been imposed upon him without his own consent; this must be the only true and proper foundation of all the governments subsisting in the world, and that to which the people who compose them have an unalienable right to bring them back.

It must necessarily be understood, therefore, whether it be expressed or not, that all people live in society for their mutual advantage; so that the good and happiness of the members, that is the majority of the members of any state, is the great standard by which every thing relating to that state must finally be determined. And though it may be supposed, that a body of people may be bound by a voluntary resignation of all their interests to a single person, or to a few, it can never be supposed that the resignation is obligatory on their posterity; because it is manifestly *contrary to the good of the whole that it should be so.*

I own it is rather matter of surprise to me, that this great object of all government should have been so little insisted on by our great writers who have treated of this subject, and that more use hath not been made of it. In treating of particular regulations in states, this principle necessarily obtruded itself; all arguments in favour of any law being always drawn from a consideration of its tendency to promote the public good; and yet it has often escaped the notice of writers in discoursing on the first principles of society, and the subject of civil and religious liberty.

This one general idea, properly pursued, throws the greatest light upon the whole system of policy, morals, and, I may add, theology too. To a mind not warped by theological and metaphysical subtilties, the divine being appears to be actuated by no other views than the noblest we can conceive, the happiness of his creatures. Virtue and right conduct consist in those affections and actions which terminate in the public good; justice and veracity, for instance, having nothing intrinsically excellent in them, separate from their relation to the happiness of mankind; and the whole system of right to power, property, and every thing else in society, must be regulated by the same consideration: the decisive question, when any of these subjects are examined, being, What is it that the good of the community requires?

Let it be observed, in this place, that I by no means assert, that the good of mankind requires a state of the most perfect political liberty. This, indeed, is not possible, except in exceeding small states; in none, perhaps, that are so large as even the republics of ancient Greece; or as Genoa, or Geneva in modern times. Such small republics as these, if they were desirable, would be impracticable; because a state of perfect equality, in communities or individuals, can never be preserved, while some are more powerful, more enterprising, and more successful in their attempts than others. And an ambitious nation could not wish for a fairer opportunity of arriving at extensive empire, than to find the neighbouring countries cantoned out into a number of small governments; which could have no power to withstand it singly, and which could never form sufficiently extensive confederacies, or act with sufficient unanimity, and expedition, to oppose it with success.

Supposing, therefore, that, in order to prevent the greatest of all inconveniences, very extensive, and consequently absolute monarchies, it may be expedient to have such states as England, France, and Spain; political liberty must, in some measure, be restrained; but *in what manner* a restraint should be put upon it, or *how far* it should extend, is not easy to be ascertained. In general, it should seem, that none but persons of considerable fortune should be capable of arriving at the highest offices in the government; not only because, all other circumstances being equal, such persons will generally have had the best education, and consequently be the best qualified to act for the public good; but because also, they will necessarily have the most property at stake, and will, therefore, be most interested in the fate of their country.

Let it be observed, however, that what may be called a *moderate* fortune (though a thing of so variable a nature cannot be defined) should be considered as equivalent in this respect, to the most affluent one. Persons who are born to a moderate fortune, are, indeed, generally better educated, have, consequently, more enlarged minds, and are, in all respects, more truly *independent*, than those who are born to great opulence.

For the same reason, it may, perhaps, be more eligible, that those who are extremely dependent should not be allowed to have votes in the nomination of the chief magistrates; because this might, in some instances, be only throwing more votes into the hands of those persons on whom they depend. But if, in every state of considerable extent, we suppose a *gradation* of elective offices, and if we likewise suppose the lowest classes of the people to have votes in the nomination of the lowest officers, and, as they increase in wealth and importance, to have a share in the choice of persons to fill the higher posts, till they themselves be admitted candidates for places of public trust; we shall, perhaps, form an idea of as much political liberty as is consistent with the state of mankind. And I think experience shows, that the highest offices of all, equivalent to that of *king*, ought to be, in some measure, hereditary, as in England; elective monarchies having generally been the theatres of cabal, confusion, and misery.

[It must be acknowledged, however, to be exceedingly hazardous to the liberties of a people, to have any office of importance frequently filled by the same persons, or their descendants. The boundaries of very great power can never be so exactly defined, but that, when it becomes the interest of men to extend them, and when so flattering an object is kept a long time in view, opportunities will be found for the purpose. What nation would not have been enslaved by the uncontroverted succession of only three such princes as Henry IV. of France, Henry VII. of England, or the present king of Prussia? The more accomplished and glorious they were as warriors, or statesmen, the more dangerous would they be as *princes*, in free states. It is nothing but the continual fear of a revolt, in favour of some rival, that could keep such princes within any bounds; i.e. that could make it their interest to court the favour of the people.

Hereditary nobles stand in the same predicament with hereditary princes. The long continuance of the same parliaments have also the same tendency. And had not these things, together with an independent ecclesiastical power, been wonderfully balanced in our constitution, it could never have stood so long. The more complex any machine is, and the more nicely it is fitted to answer its purpose, the more liable it is to disorder. The more avenues there are to arbitrary power, the more attention it requires to guard them; and with all the vigilance of the people of these nations, they have more than once been obliged to have recourse to the sword. The liberties we now enjoy, precarious as they are, have not been purchased without blood.

Though it be very evident that no office of great trust and power should be suffered to continue a long time in the same hands, the succession might be so rapid, that the remedy would be worse than the disease. With respect to this nation, it seems to be agreed, that *septennial parliaments* have brought our liberties into very eminent hazard, and that *triennial*, if not *annual* parliaments would be better. Indeed septennial parliaments were at first a direct usurpation of the rights of the people: for, by the same authority that one parliament prolonged their own power to seven years, they might have continued it to twice seven, or, like the parliament in 1641, have made it perpetual. The bulk of the people never see the most obvious tendencies of things, or so flagrant a violation of the constitution would never have been suffered. But whereas a general *clamour* might have prevented the evil, it may require something more to redress it.]

But though the exact medium of political liberty, [with respect either to the *property* of men in offices of trust, or to their *continuance in power*,] be not easily fixed, it is not of much consequence to do it; since a considerable degree of perfection in government will admit of great varieties in this respect; and the extreme of political slavery, which excludes all persons, except one, or a very few, from having access to the chief magistracy, or from having votes in the choice of magistrates, [and which keeps all the power of the state in the same hands, or the same families,] is easily marked out, and the fatal effects of it are very striking. For such is the state of mankind, that persons possessed of unbounded power will generally act as if they forgot the proper nature and design of their station, and pursue their own interest, though it be opposite to that of the community at large.

[Provided those who make laws submit to them themselves, and, with respect to taxes in particular, so long as those who impose them bear an equal share with the rest of the community, there will be no complaint. But in all cases, when those who lay the tax upon others exempt themselves, there is *tyranny*; and the man who submits to a tax of a penny, levied in this manner, is liable to have the last penny he has extorted from him.

Men of equal rank and fortune with those who usually compose the English house of Commons have nothing to fear from the imposition of taxes, so long as there is any thing like *rotation* in that office; because those who impose them are liable to pay them themselves, and are no better able to bear the burden; but persons of lower rank, and especially those who have no votes in the election of members, may have reason to fear, because an unequal part of the burden may be laid upon them. They are necessarily a *distinct order* in the community, and have no direct method of controlling the measures of the legislature. Our increasing *game-laws* have all the appearance of the haughty decrees of a tyrant, who sacrifices every thing to his own pleasure and caprice.

Upon these principles it is evident, that there must have been a gross inattention to the very first principles of liberty, to say nothing worse, in the first scheme of taxing the inhabitants of America in the British parliament.]

But if there be any truth in the principles above laid down, it must be a fundamental maxim in all governments, that if any man hold what is called a high rank, or enjoy privileges, and prerogatives in a state, it is because the good of the state requires that he should hold that rank, or enjoy those privileges; and such persons, whether they be called kings, senators, or nobles; or by whatever names, or titles, they be distinguished, are, to all intents and purposes, the *servants of the public*, and accountable to the people for the discharge of their respective offices.

If such magistrates abuse their trust, in the people, therefore, lies the right of *deposing*, and consequently of *punishing* them. And the only reason why abuses which have crept into offices have been connived at, is, that the correcting of them, by having recourse to first principles, and the people taking into their own hands their right to appoint or change their officers, and to ascertain the bounds of their authority, is far from being easy, except in small states; so that the remedy would often be worse than the disease.

But, in the largest states, if the abuses of government should, at any time be great and manifest; if the servants of the people, forgetting their *masters*, and their masters' interest, should pursue a separate one of their own; if, instead of considering that they are made for the people, they should consider the people as made for them; if the oppressions and violations of right should be great, flagrant, and universally resented; if the tyrannical governors should have no friends but a few sycophants, who had long preyed upon the vitals of their fellow citizens, and who might be expected to desert a government, whenever their interests should be detached from it: if, in consequence of these circumstances, it should become manifest, that the risk, which would be run in attempting a revolution would be trifling, and the evils which might be apprehended from it, were far less than those which were actually suffered, and which were daily increasing; in the name of God, I ask, what principles are those, which ought to restrain an injured and insulted people from asserting their natural rights, and from changing, or even punishing their governors, that is their *servants*, who had abused their trust; or from altering the whole form of their government, if it appeared to be of a structure so liable to abuse?

To say that these forms of government have been long established, and that these oppressions have been long suffered, without any complaint, is to supply the strongest argument for their abolition. Lawyers, who are governed by rules and precedents, are very apt to fall into mistakes, in determining what is right and lawful, in cases which are, in their own nature, prior to any fixed laws or precedents. The only reason for the authority of precedents and general rules in matters of law and government, is, that all persons may know what *is law*; which they could not do if the administration of it was not uniform, and the same in similar cases. But if the precedents and general rules themselves be a greater grievance than the violation of them, and the establishment of better precedents, and better general rules, what becomes of their obligation? The necessity of the thing, in the changing course of human affairs, obliges all governments to alter their general rules, and to set up new precedents in affairs of less importance; and why may not a proportionably greater necessity plead as strongly for the alteration of the most general rules, and for setting up new precedents in matters of the greatest consequence, affecting the most fundamental principles of any government, and the distribution of power among its several members?

Nothing can more justly excite the indignation of an honest and oppressed citizen, than to hear a prelate, who enjoys a considerable benefice, under a corrupt government, pleading for its support by those abominable perversions of scripture, which have been too common on this occasion; as by urging in its favour that passage of St Paul, *The powers which be are ordained of God*, and others of a similar import. It is a sufficient answer to such an absurd quotation as this, that for the same reason, the powers which *will be* will be ordained of God also.

Something, indeed, might have been said in favour of the doctrines of *passive obedience* and *non-resistance*,[4] at the time when they were first started; but a man must be infatuated who will not renounce them now. The Jesuits, about two centuries ago, in order to vindicate their king-killing principles, happened, among other arguments, to make use of this great and just principle, that *all civil power is ultimately derived from the people*: and their adversaries, in England, and elsewhere, instead of showing how they abused and perverted that fundamental principle of all government in the case in question, did, what disputants warmed with controversy are very apt to do; they denied the principle itself, and maintained that *all civil power is derived from God*, as if the Jewish theocracy had been established throughout the whole world. From this maxim it was a clear consequence, that the governments, which at any time subsist, being *the ordinance of God*,

---

[4] 'Passive obedience' or 'passive resistance' constituted the basic Lutheran version of resistance, and was often juxtaposed to the more explicit justification of rebellion offered by Calvinist theorists in the 1570s and Catholic ones in the 1580s and 1590s. For writers in early Stuart England, 'passive obedience' or 'resistance' was the only legitimate form of resistance and was again invoked by High-Churchmen in the wake of 1688.

and the kings which are at any time upon the throne, being *the vicegerents of God*, must not be opposed.

So long as there were recent examples of good kings deposed, and some of them massacred by wild enthusiasts, some indulgence might be allowed to those warm, but weak friends of society, who would lay hold of any principle, which, however ill founded, would supply an argument for more effectually preserving the public peace; but to maintain the same absurd principles at this day, when the danger from which they served to shelter us is over, and the heat of controversy is abated, shows the strongest and most blameable prepossession. Writers in defence of them do not deserve a serious answer: and to allege those principles in favour of a corrupt government, which nothing can excuse but their being brought in favour of a good one, is unpardonable.

The history of this controversy about the doctrine of passive obedience and non-resistance, affords a striking example of the danger of having recourse to false principles in controversy. They may serve a particular turn, but, in other cases, may be capable of the most dangerous application; whereas universal truth will, in all possible cases, have the best consequences, and be ever favourable to the true interests of mankind.

It will be said, that it is opening a door to *rebellion*, to assert that magistrates, abusing their power, may be set aside by the people, who are of course their own judges when that power is abused. May not the people, it is said, abuse their power, as well as their governors? I answer, it is very possible they may abuse their power: it is possible they may imagine themselves oppressed when they are not: it is possible that their animosity may be artfully and unreasonably inflamed, by ambitious and enterprising men, whose views are often best answered by popular tumults and insurrections; and the people may suffer in consequence of their folly and precipitancy. But what man is there, or what body of men (whose right to direct their own conduct was never called in question) but are liable to be imposed upon, and to suffer in consequence of their mistaken apprehensions and precipitate conduct?

With respect to large societies, it is very improbable, that the people should be too soon alarmed, so as to be driven to these extremities. In such cases, the power of the government, that is, of the governors, must be very extensive and arbitrary; and the power of the people scattered, and difficult to be united; so that, if a man have common sense, he will see it to be madness to propose, or to lay any measures for a general insurrection against the government, except in case of very general and great oppression. Even patriots, in such circumstances, will consider, that present evils always appear greater in consequence of their being present; but that the future evils of a revolt, and a temporary anarchy, may be much greater than are apprehended at a distance. They will, also, consider, that unless their measures be perfectly well laid, and their success decisive, ending in a change, not of *men*, but of *things*; not of governors, but of the rules and administration of government, they will only rivet their chains the faster, and bring upon themselves and their country tenfold ruin.

So obvious are these difficulties, that lie in the way of procuring redress of grievances by force of arms, that I think we may say, without exception, that in all cases of hostile opposition to government, the people must have been in the right; and that nothing but very great oppression could drive them to such desperate measures. The bulk of a people seldom so much as *complain* without reason, because they never think of complaining till they *feel*; so that, in all cases of dissatisfaction with government, it is most probable, that the people are injured.

The case, I own, may be otherwise in states of small extent, where the power of the governors is comparatively small, and the power of the people great, and soon united. These fears, therefore, may be prudent in Venice, in Genoa, or in the small cantons of Switzerland; but it were to the last degree, absurd to extend them to Great-Britain.

The English history will inform us, that the people of this country have always borne extreme oppression, for a long time before there has appeared any danger of a general insurrection against the government. What a series of encroachments upon their rights did even the feudal barons, whose number was not very considerable, and whose power was great, bear from William the Conqueror, and his successors, before they broke out into actual rebellion on that account, as in the reigns of king John, and Henry the third![5] And how much were the lowest orders of the poor commons trampled upon with impunity by both, till a much later period; when, all the while, they were so far from attempting any resistance, or even complaining of the gross

[5] The baronial rebellion against John resulted in the Magna Carta (1215), and that against Henry III in the Provisions of Oxford (1258).

infringements of their rights, that they had not so much as the idea of their having any rights to be trampled upon! After the people had begun to acquire property, independence, and an idea of their natural rights, how long did they bear a load of old and new oppressions under the Tudors, but more especially under the Stuarts, before they broke out into what the friends of arbitrary power affect to call *the grand rebellion*! And how great did that obstinate civil war show the power of the king to be, notwithstanding the most intolerable and wanton abuse of it! At the close of the year 1642, it was more probable that the king would have prevailed than the parliament; and his success would have been certain, if his conduct had not been as weak, as it was wicked.

So great was the power of the crown, that after the restoration, Charles the second was tempted to act the same part with his father, and actually did it, in a great measure, with impunity; till, at last, he was even able to reign without parliaments; and if he had lived much longer, he would, in all probability, have been as arbitrary as the king of France. His brother James the second, had almost subverted both the civil and religious liberties of his country, in the short space of four years, and might have done it completely, if he could have been content to have proceeded with more caution; nay, he might have succeeded notwithstanding his precipitancy, if the divine being had not, at that critical time, raised up William the third, of glorious memory, for our deliverance. But, God be thanked, the government of this country, is now fixed upon so good and firm a basis, and is so generally acquiesced in, that they are only the mere tools of a court party, or the narrow minded bigots among the inferior clergy, who, to serve their own low purposes, do now and then promote the cry, that the church or the state is in danger.

As to what is called the crime of *rebellion*, we have nothing to do either with the name, or the thing, in the case before us. That term, if it admit of any definition, is an attempt to subvert a lawful government; but the question is, whether an oppressive government, though it have been ever so long established, can be a lawful one; or, to cut off all dispute about words, if lawful, legal, and constitutional, be maintained to be the same thing, whether the lawful, legal, and constitutional government be a *good* government, or one in which sufficient provision is made for the happiness of the subjects of it. If it fail in this essential character, respecting the true end and object of all civil government, no other property or title, with which it may be dignified, ought to shelter it from the generous attack of the noble and daring patriot. If the bold attempt be precipitate, and unsuccessful, the tyrannical government, will be sure to term it rebellion, but that censure cannot make the thing itself less glorious. The memory of such brave, though unsuccessful and unfortunate friends of liberty, and of the rights of mankind, as that of Harmodius and Aristogiton among the Athenians, and Russel and Sidney in our own country,[6] — will be had in everlasting honour by their grateful fellow citizens; and history will speak another language than laws.

If it be asked how far a people may lawfully go in punishing their chief magistrates, I answer that, if the enormity of the offence (which is of the same extent as the injury done to the public) be considered, any punishment is justifiable that a man can incur in human society. It may be said, there are no laws to punish those governors, and we must not condemn persons by laws made *ex post facto*; for this conduct will vindicate the most obnoxious measures of the most tyrannical administration. But I answer, that this is a case, in its own nature, prior to the establishment of any laws whatever; as it affects the very being of society, and defeats the principal ends for which recourse was originally had to it. There may be no fixed law against an open invader, who should attempt to seize upon a country, with a view to enslave all its inhabitants; but must not the invader be apprehended, and even put to death, though he have broken no express law then in being, or none of which he was properly apprized? And why should a man, who takes the advantage of his being king, or governor, to subvert the laws and liberties of his country, be considered in any other light than that of a foreign invader? Nay his crime is much more atrocious, as he was appointed the guardian of the laws and liberties, which he subverts, and which he was, therefore, under the strongest obligation to maintain.

In a case, therefore, of this highly criminal nature, *salus populi suprema est lex*. That must be done which the good of the whole requires; and, generally, kings deposed, banished, or imprisoned, are

---

[6] Harmodius and Aristogiton were the killers of the Athenian tyrant Hipparchus in 514 BC; William Russell and Algernon Sidney were the republican martyrs executed by Charles II for complicity in the abortive Rye House Plot in 1683.

highly dangerous to a nation; because, let them have governed ever so ill, it will be the interest of some to be their partisans, and to attach themselves to their cause.

It will be supposed, that these observations have a reference to what passed in England in the year 1648. Let it be supposed. Surely a man, and an Englishman, may be at liberty to give his opinion, freely and without disguise, concerning a transaction of so old a date. Charles the first, whatever he was in his private character, which is out of the question here, was certainly a very bad king of England. During a course of many years, and notwithstanding repeated remonstrances, he governed by maxims utterly subversive of the fundamental and free constitution of this country; and, therefore, he deserved the severest punishment. If he was misled by his education, or his friends, he was, like any other criminal, in the same circumstances, to be pitied, but by no means to be spared on that account.

From the nature of things it was necessary that the opposition should begin from a few, who may, therefore, be stiled a *faction*; but after the civil war (which necessarily ensued from the king's obstinacy, and in which he had given repeated instances of dissimulation and treachery) there was evidently no safety, either for the faction or the nation, short of his death. It is to be regretted, that the situation of things was such, that the sentence could not be passed by the whole nation, or their representatives, solemnly assembled for that purpose. I am sensible indeed, that the generality of the nation, at that time, would not have voted the death of their sovereign; but this was not owing to any want of a just sense of the wrongs he had done them, but to an opinion of the *sacredness of kingly power*, from which very few of the friends of liberty in those times, especially among the Presbyterians, who were the majority, could intirely divest themselves. Such a transaction would have been an immortal honour to this country, whenever that superstitious notion shall be obliterated: A notion which has been extremely useful in the infant state of societies; but which, like other superstitions, subsists long after it hath ceased to be of use.

The sum of what hath been advanced upon this head, is a maxim, than which nothing is more true, that *every government, in its original principles, and antecedent to its present form, is an equal republic*; and, consequently, that every man, when he comes to be sensible of his natural rights, and to feel his own importance, will consider himself as fully equal to any other person whatever. The consideration of riches and power, however acquired, must be entirely set aside, when we come to these first principles. The very idea of property, or right of any kind, is founded upon a regard to the general good of the society, under whose protection it is enjoyed; and nothing is properly *a man's own*, but what general rules, which have for their object the good of the whole, give to him. To whomsoever the society delegates its power, it is delegated to them for the more easy management of public affairs, and in order to make the more effectual provision for the happiness of the whole. Whoever enjoys property, or riches in the state, enjoys them for the good of the state, as well as for himself; and whenever those powers, riches, or rights of any kind, are abused, to the injury of the whole, that awful and ultimate tribunal, in which every citizen hath an equal voice, may demand the resignation of them; and in circumstances, where regular commissions from this abused public cannot be had, every man, who has power, and who is actuated with the sentiments of the public, may assume a public character, and bravely redress public wrongs. In such dismal and critical circumstances, the stifled voice of an oppressed country is a loud call upon every man, possessed with a spirit of patriotism, to exert himself; and whenever that voice shall be at liberty, it will ratify and applaud the action, which it could not formally authorize.

In large states, this ultimate seat of power, this tribunal to which lies an appeal from every other, and from which no appeal can even be imagined, is too much hid, and kept out of sight by the present complex forms of government, which derive their authority from it. Hence hath arisen a want of clearness and consistency in the language of the friends of liberty. Hence the preposterous and slavish maxim, that whatever is enacted by that body of men, in whom the supreme power of the state is vested, must, in all cases, be implicitly obeyed; and that no attempt to repeal an unjust law can be vindicated, beyond a simple remonstrance addressed to the legislators. A case, which is very intelligible, but which can never happen, will demonstrate the absurdity of such a maxim.

Suppose the king of England, and the two houses of parliament, should make a law, in all the usual forms, to exempt the members of either house from paying taxes to the government, or to take to themselves the property of their fellow citizens. A law like this would open the eyes of the whole nation, and show them the true principles of government, and the power of governors. The nation would see that the most regular governments may become tyrannical, and their governors oppressive, by separating their interest from that of the people whom they govern. Such a law would show them to be but servants, and servants who had shamefully abused their trust. In such a case, every man for himself would lay his hand upon his sword, and the authority of the supreme power of the state would be annihilated.

So plain are these first principles of all government, and political liberty, that I will take upon me to say, it is impossible a man should not be convinced of them, who brings to the subject a mind free from the grossest and meanest prejudices. Whatever be the form of any government, whoever be the supreme magistrates, or whatever be their number; that is, to whomsoever the power of the society is delegated, their authority is, in its own nature, reversible. No man can be supposed to resign his natural liberty, but on *conditions*. These conditions, whether they be expressed or not, must be violated, whenever the plain and obvious ends of government are not answered; and a delegated power, perverted from the intention for which it was bestowed, expires of course. Magistrates therefore, who consult not the good of the public, and who employ their power to oppress the people, are a public nuisance, and their power is abrogated *ipso facto*.

This, however, can only be the case in extreme oppression; when the blessings of society and civil government, great and important as they are, are bought too dear; when it is better not to be governed at all, than to be governed in such a manner; or, at least, when the hazard of a change of government would be apparently the less evil of the two; and, therefore, these occasions rarely occur in the course of human affairs. It may be asked, what should a people do in case of less general oppression, and only particular grievances; when the deputies of the people make laws which evidently favour themselves, and bear hard upon the body of the people they represent, and such as they would certainly disapprove, could they be assembled for that purpose? I answer, that when this appears to be very clearly the case, as it ought by all means to do (since, in many cases, if the government have not power to enforce a bad law, it will not have power to enforce a good one) the first step which a wise and moderate people will take, is to make a remonstrance to the legislature; and if that be not practicable, or be not heard; still, if the complaints be general, and loud, a wise prince and ministry will pay regard to them; or they will, at length, be weary of enforcing a penal law which is generally abhorred and disregarded; when they see the people will run the risk of the punishment, if it cannot be evaded, rather than quietly submit to the injunction. And a regard to the good of society will certainly justify this conduct of the people.

If an over scrupulous conscience should prevent the people from expressing their sentiments in this manner, there is no method left, until an opportunity offers of choosing honester deputies, in which the voice of the lowest classes can be heard, in order to obtain the repeal of an oppressive law.

Governors will never be awed by the voice of the people, so long as it is a mere voice, without overt-acts. The consequence of these seemingly moderate maxims is, that a door will be left open to all kinds of oppression, without any resource or redress, till the public wrongs be accumulated to the degree above mentioned, when all the world would justify the utter subversion of the government. These maxims, therefore, admit of no remedy but the last, and most hazardous of all. But is not even a mob a less evil than a rebellion, and ought the former to be so severely blamed by writers on this subject, when it may prevent the latter? Of two evils of any kind, political as well as others, it is the dictate of common sense to choose the less. Besides, according to common notions, avowed by writers upon morals on less general principles, and by lawyers too, all penal laws give a man an alternative, either to abstain from the action prohibited, or to take the penalty.

SECTION III.

Of Civil Liberty

Sect. I.

Of the nature of Civil Liberty in general.

It is a matter of the greatest importance, that we carefully distinguish between the *form* and the *extent of power* in a government; for many maxims in politics depend upon the one, which are too generally ascribed to the other.

It is comparatively of small consequence, *who*, or *how many* be our governors, or *how long* their office continues, provided their power be the same while they are in office, and the administration be uniform and certain. All the difference which can arise to states from diversities, in the number or continuance of governors, can only flow from the motives and opportunities, which those different circumstances may give their deputies, of extending, or making a bad use of their power. But whether a people enjoy more or fewer of their natural rights, under any form of government, is a matter of the last importance; and upon this depends, what, I should choose to call, the *civil liberty* of the state, as distinct from its *political liberty*.

If the power of government be very extensive, and the subjects of it have, consequently, little power over their own actions, that government is tyrannical, and oppressive; whether, with respect to its form, it be a monarchy, an aristocracy, or even a republic. For the government of the temporary magistrates of a democracy, or even the laws themselves may be as tyrannical as the maxims of the most despotic monarchy, and the administration of the government may be as destructive of private happiness. The only consolation that a democracy suggests in those circumstances is, that every member of the state has a chance of arriving at a share in the chief magistracy, and consequently of playing the tyrant in his turn; and as there is no government in the world so perfectly democratical, as that every member of the state, without exception, has a right of being admitted into the administration, great numbers will be in the same condition as if they had lived under the most absolute monarchy; and this is, in fact, almost universally the case with the poor, in all governments.

For the same reason, if there were no fixed laws, but every thing was decided according to the will of the persons in power; who is there that would think it of much consequence, whether his life, his liberty, or his property were at the mercy of one, of a few, or of a great number of people, that is, of a mob, liable to the worst of influences. So far, therefore, we may safely say, with Mr Pope, that *those governments which are best administered are best:*[7] – that is, provided the power of government be moderate, and leave a man the most valuable of his private rights; provided the laws be certainly known to every one, and the administration of them be uniform, it is of no consequence how many, or how few persons are employed in the administration. But it must be allowed, that there is not the same chance for the continuance of such laws, and of such an administration, whether the power be lodged in few, or in more hands.

The governments now subsisting in Europe differ widely in their forms; but it is certain, that the present happiness of the subjects of them can by no means be estimated by a regard to that circumstance only. It depends chiefly upon the power, the extent, and the maxims of government, respecting personal security, private property, &c. and on the certainty and uniformity of the administration.

Civil liberty has been greatly impaired by an abuse of the maxim, that the joint understanding of all the members of a state, properly collected, must be preferable to that of individuals; and consequently that the more the cases are, in which mankind are governed by this united reason of the whole community, so much the better; whereas, in truth, the greater part of human actions are of such a nature, that more inconvenience would follow from their being fixed by laws, than from their being left to every man's arbitrary will.

[We may be assisted in conceiving the nature of this species of liberty, by considering what it is that men propose to gain by entering into society. Now it is evident, that we are not led to wish for a state of society by the want of any thing that we can conveniently procure for ourselves. As a man, and a member of civil society, I am desirous to receive such assistance as *numbers* can give to *individuals*, but by no means that assistance which numbers, as such, cannot give to individuals; and, least of all, such as individuals are better qualified to impart to numbers. There are many things respecting human happiness that properly fall under the two last mentioned classes, and the great difficulty concerning the due extent of civil government lies in distinguishing the objects that belong to these classes. Little difficulty, however, has, in fact, arisen from the nature of the things, in comparison of the difficulties that have been occasioned by its being the interest of men to combine, confound, and perplex them.

As far as mere *strength* can go, it is evident, that *numbers* may assist an individual, and this seems to have been the first, if not the only reason for having recourse to society. If I be injured, and not able to redress my own wrongs, I ask help of my neighbours and acquaintance; and occasions may arise, in which the more assistance I can procure, the better. But I can seldom want the assistance of numbers in managing my domestic affairs, which require nothing but my own constant inspection, and the immediate application of my own faculties. In this case, therefore, any attempt of numbers to assist me, would only occasion embarrassment and distress.

For the purpose of finding out *truth*, individuals are always employed to assist multitudes; for, notwithstanding it be probable, that more discoveries will be made by a number of persons than by one person; and though one person may assist another in suggesting and perfecting any improvements in science; yet still they all act as *independent individuals*, giving voluntary information and advice. For whenever numbers have truth or knowledge for their object, and act as a collective body, i.e. *authoritatively*, so that no single person can have power to determine any thing till the majority have been brought to agree to it, the interests of knowledge will certainly suffer, there is so little prospect of the prejudices of the many giving way to the better judgment of an individual. Here, there is a case, in which society must always be benefited by individuals, as such, and not by numbers, in a collective capacity. It is least of all, therefore, for the advancement of knowledge, that I should be induced to wish for the authoritative interposition of society.

In this manner it might not be a very difficult thing, for candid and impartial persons, to fix reasonable bounds for the interposition of laws and government. They are defective when they leave an individual destitute of that assistance which they could procure for him, and they are burdensome and oppressive; i. e. injurious to the natural rights and civil liberties of mankind, when they lay a man under unnecessary restrictions, by controlling his conduct, and preventing him from serving himself, with respect to those things, in which they can yield him no real assistance, and in providing for which he is in no danger of injuring others.

This question may be farther illustrated by two pretty just comparisons. Magistrates are the *servants* of the public, and therefore the use of them may be illustrated by that of servants. Now let a man's fortune or his incapacity be such that his dependence on servants is ever so great; there must be many things that he will be obliged to do for himself, and in which any attempt to assist him would only embarrass and distress him; and in many cases in which persons *do* make use of servants, they would be much more at their ease, if their situation would allow them to do without their assistance. If magistrates be considered in the more respectable light of *representatives* and *deputies* of the people, it should likewise be considered, that there are many cases, in which it is more convenient for a man to act *in person* than by any deputation whatever.

In some respects, however, it must be acknowledged, that the proper extent of civil government is not easily circumscribed within exact limits. That the happiness of the whole community is the ultimate end of government can never be doubted, and all claims of individuals inconsistent with the public good are absolutely null and void; but there is a real difficulty in determining what general rules, respecting the extent of the power of government, or of governors, are most conducive to the public good.]

Some may think it best, that the legislature should make express provision for every thing which can even indirectly, remotely, and consequentially, affect the public good; while others may think it best, that every thing, which is not properly of a civil nature, should be entirely overlooked by the civil magistrate; that it is for the advantage of the society, upon the whole, that all those things be left to take their own natural course, and that the legislature cannot interfere in them, without defeating its own great object, the public good.

We are so little capable of arguing *a priori* in matters of government, that it should seem, experiments only can determine how far this power of the legislature ought to extend; and it should likewise seem, that, till a sufficient number of experiments have been made, it becomes the wisdom of the civil magistracy to take as little upon its hands as possible, and never to interfere, without the greatest caution, in things that do not immediately affect the lives, liberty, or property of the members of the community; that civil magistrates should hardly ever be moved to exert themselves by the mere *tendencies of things*, those tendencies are generally so vague, and often so imaginary; and that nothing but a manifest and urgent necessity (of which, however, themselves are, to be sure, the only judges) can justify them in extending their authority to whatever has no more than a tendency, though the strongest possible, to disturb the tranquility and happiness of the state.

There can be no doubt but that any people, forming themselves into a society, may subject themselves to whatever restrictions they please; and consequently, that the supreme civil magistrates, on whom the whole power of the society is devolved, may make what laws they please; but the question is, what restrictions and laws are wise, and calculated to promote the public good; for such only are just, right, and, properly speaking, lawful.

Political and civil liberty, as before explained, though very different, have, however, a very near and manifest connection; and the former is the chief guard of the latter, and on that account, principally, it is valuable, and worth contending for. If all the political power of this country were lodged in the hands of one person, and the government thereby changed into an absolute monarchy, the people would find no difference, provided the same laws, and the same administration, which now subsist, were continued. But then, the people, having no political liberty, would have no *security* for the continuance of the same laws, and the same administration. They would have no guard for their civil liberty. The monarch, having it in his option, might not choose to continue the same laws, and the same administration. He might fancy it to be for his own interest to alter them, and to abridge his subjects in their private rights; and, in general, it may be depended upon, that governors will not consult the interest of the people, except it be their own interest too, because governors are but men. But while a number of the people have a share in the legislature, so as to be able to control the supreme magistrate, there is a great probability that things will continue in a good state. For the more political liberty the people have, the safer is their civil liberty.

[There may, however, be some kind of guard for civil liberty, independent of that which is properly called *political*. For the supreme magistrate, though *nominally*, he have all the power of the state in his hands, and, without violating any of the forms of the constitution, may enact and execute what laws he pleases; yet his circumstances may be such, as shall lay him under what is equivalent to a natural *impossibility* of doing what he would choose. And I do not here mean that kind of restraint, which all arbitrary princes are under, from the fear of a revolt of their subjects; which is often the consequence of great oppression; but from what may be called *the spirit of the times*.

Magistrates, being men, cannot but have, in some measure, the feelings of other men. They could not, therefore, be happy themselves, if they were conscious that their conduct exposed them to universal hatred and contempt. Neither can they be altogether indifferent to the light in which their characters and conduct will appear to posterity. For their own sakes, therefore, they will generally pay some regard to the sentiments of their people.

The more civilized any country is, the more effectual will this kind of guard to political liberty prove; because, in those circumstances, a sense of justice and honour have got firmer hold of the minds of men; so that a violation of them would be more sensibly felt, and more generally and strongly resented. For this reason, a gentleman of fashion and fortune has much less to dread in France, or in Denmark, than in Turkey. The confiscation of an overgrown rich man's effects, without any cause assigned, would make no great noise in the latter; whereas in those countries, in which the *forms* of law and liberty have been long established, they necessarily carry with them more or less of the *substance* also.[8]

There is not, I believe, any country in Europe, in which a man could be condemned, and his effects confiscated, but a crime must be alleged, and a process of law be gone through. The confirmed habit of thinking in these countries is such, that no prince could dispense with these formalities. He would be deemed *insane*, if he should attempt to do otherwise; the succession would be set aside in favour of the next heir, by the general consent of the people, and the revolution would

---

[8] See Hume's discussion of the 'civilized monarchy' in his essay 'Of the Rise and Progress of the Arts and Sciences', *Essays*, edited by Eugene F. Miller (Indianapolis, 1985).

take place without blood shed. No person standing near any European prince would hesitate what to do, if his sovereign should attempt to cut off a man's head, out of mere wantonness and sport, a thing that would only strike the beholders with awe in some foreign courts.

Should the English government become arbitrary, and the people, disgusted with the conduct of their parliaments, do what the people of Denmark have done, choose their sovereign for their perpetual representative, and surrender into his hands all the power of state; the forms of a free government have been so long established, that the most artful tyrant would be a long time before he could render life and property as precarious as it is even in France. The trial by *juries*, in ordinary cases, would stand a long time; the *habeas corpus* would, generally at least, continue in force, and all executions would be in public.

It may be questioned whether the progress to absolute slavery and insecurity would be more rapid, if the king were *nominally* arbitrary, or only *virtually* so, by uniformly influencing the house of Commons.

In some respects, so large a body of men would venture upon things which no single person would choose to do of his own authority; and so long as they had little intercourse but with one another, they would not be much affected with the sense of fear or shame. One may safely say, that no single member of the house would have had the assurance to decide as the majority have often done, in cases of controverted elections.

But, on the other hand, as the members of the house of Commons necessarily spend a great part of the summer months with their friends in the country, they could not show their faces after passing an act, by which gentlemen like themselves, or even their electors, should be much aggrieved; though they may now and then oppress the poor by unreasonable game acts, &c. because they never converse with any of the poor except their immediate dependants, who would not choose to remonstrate on the subject.

Besides, so long as the members of parliament are *elected*, though only once in seven years, those of them that are really chosen by the people can have no chance of being re-elected but by pleasing the people; and many of them would not choose to reduce themselves and their posterity, out of the house, to a worse condition than they originally were. Let them be ever so obsequious to a court, they will hardly choose to deprive themselves of all power of giving any thing for the future.

Independent, therefore, of all conviction of mind, there must be a *minority* in the house, whose clamour and opposition will impede the progress of tyranny; whereas a king, surrounded by his guards, and a cringing nobility, has no check. If, however, he be a man of sense, and read history, he may comprehend the various causes of the extreme insecurity of despotic princes; many of whom have appeared in all the pomp of power in the morning, and have been in prison, without eyes, or massacred, and dragged about the streets before night.

At all adventures, I should think it more wise to bear with a tyrannical parliament, though a more expensive mode of servitude for the present, than an arbitrary prince. So long as there is a power that can *nominally* put a negative upon the proceedings of the court, there is some chance, that circumstances may arise, in which the prince may not be able to influence them. They may see the *necessity*, if not the *wisdom* of complying with the just desires of the people; and by passing a few fundamentally good laws, true freedom may be established for ages; whereas, were the old forms of constitutional liberty once abolished, as in France, there would be little hope of their revival.

Whenever the house of Commons shall be so abandonedly corrupt, as to join with the court in abolishing any of the *essential forms of the constitution*, or effectually defeating the great purposes of it, let every Englishman, before it be too late, re-peruse the history of his country, and do what Englishmen are renowned for having formerly done in the same circumstances.]

Where civil liberty is intirely divested of its natural guard, political liberty, I should not hesitate to prefer the government of *one*, to that of a *number*; because a sense of shame would have less influence upon them, and they would keep one another in countenance, in cases in which any single person would yield to the sense of the majority.

Political and civil liberty have many things in common, which indeed, is the reason why they have been so often confounded. A sense both of political and civil slavery, makes a man think meanly of himself. The feeling of his insignificance debases his mind, checks every great and enterprising sentiment; and, in fact, renders him that poor abject creature, which he fancies himself to be. Having always some unknown evil to fear, though it should never come, he has no perfect enjoyment of himself, or of any of the blessings of life; and thus, his sentiments and his enjoyments being of a lower kind, the man sinks nearer to the state of the brute creation.

On the other hand, a sense of political and civil liberty, though there should be no great occasion to exert it in the course of a man's life, gives him a constant feeling of his own power and importance; and is the foundation of his indulging a free, bold, and manly turn of thinking, unrestrained by the most distant idea of control. Being free from all fear, he has the most perfect enjoyment of himself, and of all the blessings of life; and his sentiments and enjoyments, being raised, his very *being* is exalted, and the man makes nearer approaches to superior natures.

[Without a spirit of liberty, and a feeling of security and independence, no great improvements in agriculture, or any thing else, will ever be made by men. A man has but poor encouragement to bestow labour and expense upon a piece of ground, in which he has no secure property; and when neither himself, nor his posterity, will, probably, ever derive any permanent advantage from it. In confirmation of this, I cannot help quoting a few instructive passages from Mr *Du Poivre's Travels of a Philosopher.*[9]

It is his general observation, that "a country poorly cultivated is always inhabited by men barbarous, or oppressed." p. 5.

"In a terrestrial paradise, the Siamese are, perhaps, the most wretched people in the world. The government is despotic. The sovereign alone enjoys the true liberty which is natural to all mankind. His subjects are all slaves. Every one of them is annually taxed at six months personal service, without wages, and even without food." p. 56.

On the other hand, "The Chinese enjoy, undisturbed, their private possessions, as well as those which, being by their nature indivisible, belong to all; and he who buys a field, or receives it by inheritance from his ancestors, is of course the sole lord or master. The lands are free as the people, without feudal services, or fines of alienation. A tenth part of the produce of the earth is the only tax, or tribute, in the Chinese empire, since the origin of the monarchy. And such is the happy respect which the Chinese have for their ancient customs, that no emperor of China ever entertains the most distant thought of

---

[9] Pierre Poivre, *Voyage d'un Philosophe, ou observations sur les moeurs . . . des peuples de l'Afrique, de l'Asie* (1768; translated 1769).

augmenting it, nor his subjects the least apprehension of such augmentation." p. 78.

In arbitrary governments the *poor* are certainly the most safe, as their condition exhibits nothing that can attract the notice, or tempt the violence of a tyrant. If, therefore, a man aspire to nothing more than to get his bread by the labour of his hands, in some customary employment, he has little to fear, let him live where he will. Like the ass in the fable, he can but bear his burden. No governments can do without labourers and artisans. It is their interest to protect them, and especially those who are dexterous in the more elegant arts, that are subservient to luxury.

But the poorest can hardly be without some degree of ambition, except when that generous principle has been long repressed, and in a manner eradicated by a continual habit of slavery; and the moment that a man thinks of rendering himself in any respect conspicuous, for his wealth, knowledge, or influence of any kind, he begins to be in danger. If he have but a very handsome wife, he must not live near a despotic court, or in the neighbourhood of any great man who is countenanced by it. If he have wealth, he must hide it, and enjoy it in secret, with fear and trembling; and if he have sense, and think differently from his neighbours, he must do the same, or risk the fate of Galileo.]

I shall close this section with a few extracts from travellers, and other writers, which show the importance of political and civil liberty.

"In travelling through Germany," says Lady M. W. Montague, "it is impossible not to observe the difference between the free towns, and those under the government of absolute princes, as all the little sovereigns of Germany are. In the first there appears an air of commerce and plenty, the streets are well built, and full of people, the shops are loaded with merchandize, and the commonalty are clean and cheerful. In the other, you see a sort of shabby finery, a number of people of quality tawdried out, narrow nasty streets, out of repair, wretchedly thin of inhabitants, and above half of the common people asking alms." *Lady M. W. Montague's Letters*, vol. I. page 16.[10]

"Every house in Turkey," the same excellent writer observes, "at the death of its master, is at the grand seignior's disposal; and therefore no man cares to make a great expense, which he is not sure his

[10] *Letters of the Right Honourable Lady M—y W——-y M——-u [Mary Wortley Montagu], written during her travels* (1763).

family will be the better for. All their design is to build a house commodious, and that will last their lives, and they are very indifferent if it falls down the next year." Ib. p. 70.

"The fear of the laws," says the admirable author of the *Essay on crimes and punishments*,[11] "is salutary, but the fear of man is a fruitful and fatal source of crimes. Men enslaved are more voluptuous, more debauched, and more cruel than those who are in a state of freedom. These study the sciences, and the interests of nations. They have great objects before their eyes, and imitate them. But those whose views are confined to the present moment, endeavour, amidst the distraction of riot and debauchery, to forget their situation. Accustomed to the uncertainty of all events, the consequences of their crimes become problematical; which gives an additional force to the strength of their passions." P. 166.

"The Turkish Bashaw once destroyed all the sugar canes in Cyprus, to prevent the people having too much wealth. This island is to this day the clearest proof that can be given, how much a bad government may defeat all the kind intentions of nature: for, in spite of all the advantages a country can possibly have, there never was a more desolate place than this island is at this day." Thevenot in Knox's collection, vol. 6, p. 71.[12]

There is hardly any greater instance of the wanton abuse of power, in the invasion of the natural rights of mankind, than in the *game laws*, that are in force in different states of Europe. England has just and great complaint to make on this subject; but we are not yet reduced to the deplorable condition of the Saxons, as it is described by Hanway, vol. I. p. 433.[13]

"Hunting is the ruling passion of the Saxon court, and fatal to the inhabitants. In the hard winter of 1740, it is computed, that above 30,000 deer died in the electorate of Saxony; and yet, in the open lands and forests, there are now reckoned to remain above that number, of which no person dares kill one, under the penalty of being condemned to the gallies. In every town of any note, there are fifty of the inhabitants, who watch, five every night, by rotation, and use bells

[11] Cesare Beccaria, *Dei delitti e delle pene*, translated as *An Essay on Crimes and Punishments* (1767).
[12] Jean de Thevenot, *Relation d'un voyage fait au Levant, dans laquelle il est . . . traicté des estats sujets au Grand Segneur* (1664–84).
[13] Jonas Hanway, *A Compendium of the Travels of Mr Hanway, Sir John Mandevile and Mr Lionel Wafer, and a Description of Greenland* (London [1770]).

to frighten the deer, and defend their corn. Frequent remonstrances have been made to the court on this subject; but to no other purpose, than to convince the people of their slavery."

Felix. quem faciunt, aliena pericula cautum.[14]

SECTION IV.

In what manner an authoritative code of education would affect political and civil liberty.

Having considered the nature of civil liberty in general, I shall treat of two capital branches of which it consists. These are the rights of education, and religion. On these two articles much of the happiness of human life is acknowledged to depend; but they appear to me to be of such a nature, that the advantage we derive from them will be more effectually secured, when they are conducted by individuals, than by the state; and if this can be demonstrated, nothing more is necessary, to prove that the civil magistrate has no business to interfere with them.

This I cannot help thinking to be the shortest, and the best issue upon which we can put every thing in which the civil magistrate pretends to a right of interference. If it be probable that the business, whatever it be, will be conducted better, that is, more to the advantage of society, in his hands, than in those of individuals, the right will be allowed. In those circumstances, it is evident, that no friend to society can deny his claim. But if the nature of the thing be such, that the attention of individuals, with respect to it, can be applied to more advantage than that of the magistrate; the claim of the former must be admitted, in preference to that of the latter.

[14] 'Happy is he whom the perils of others makes cautious'.

No doubt, there are examples of both kinds. The avenging of injuries, or redressing of private wrongs, is certainly better trusted in the hands of the magistrate than in those of private persons; but with what advantage could a magistrate interfere in a thousand particulars relating to private families, and private friendships? Now I think it is clear, that education must be ranked in the latter class, or among those things in which the civil magistrate has no right to interfere; because he cannot do it to any good purpose. But since Dr Brown has lately maintained the contrary, in a treatise, intitled, *Thoughts on civil liberty, licentiousness, and faction*, and in an *Appendix relative to a proposed code of education*, subjoined to a *Sermon on the female character and education*. I shall in this section, reply to what he has advanced on this subject, and offer what has occurred to me with relation to it.

Lest it should be apprehended, that I mistake the views of this writer, I shall subjoin a few extracts from the work, which contain the substance of what he has advanced on the subject of education. He asserts, "That, the first and best security of civil liberty consists, in impressing the infant mind with such habits of thought and action, as may correspond with, and promote the appointments of public law." In his appendix, he says, that, "by a CODE OF EDUCATION, he means a system of principles, religious, moral, and political, whose tendency may be the preservation of the blessings of society, as they are enjoyed in a free state, to be instilled effectually into the infant and growing minds of the community, for this great end of public happiness."

In what manner the security of civil liberty is to be effected by means of this code of education, may be seen in the following description he gives of the institutions of Sparta. "No father had a right to educate his children according to the caprice of his own fancy. They were delivered to public officers, who initiated them early in the manners, the maxims, the exercises, the toils; in a word, in all the mental and bodily acquirements and habits which corresponded with the genius of the state. Family connections had no place. The first and leading object of their affection was the general welfare. This tuition was carefully continued till they were enrolled in the list of men."

With respect to the Athenian government, he says, page 62, "The first and ruling defect in the institution of this republic seems to have been the total want of an established education, suitable to the genius of the state. There appears not to have been any public, regular, or prescribed appointment of this kind, beyond what custom had accidentally introduced."

He says, page 70, "There were three fatal circumstances admitted into the very essence of the Roman republic, which contained the seeds of certain ruin; the first of which was, the neglect of instituting public laws, by which the education of their children might have been ascertained."

He complains, page 83, "that the British system of policy and religion is not upheld in its native power like that of Sparta, by correspondent and effectual rules of education; that it is in the power of every private man to educate his child, not only without a reverence for these, but in absolute contempt of them; that, at the revolution, p. 90, the education of youth was still left in an imperfect state; this great revolution having confined itself to the reform of public institutions, without ascending to the great fountain of political security, the private and effectual formation of the infant mind; and, p. 107, that education was afterwards left still more and more imperfect."

Lastly, he asserts, p. 156, "that the chief and essential remedy of licentiousness and faction, the fundamental means of the lasting and secure establishment of civil liberty, can only be in a general and prescribed improvement of the laws of education, to which all the members of the community should legally submit; and that for want of a prescribed code of education, the manners and principles, on which alone the state can rest, are ineffectually instilled, are vague, fluctuating and self contradictory. Nothing," he says, "is more evident, than that some reform in this great point is necessary for the security of public freedom; and that though it is an incurable defect of our political state, that it has not a correspondent and adequate code of education inwrought into its first essence; we may yet hope, that, in a secondary and inferior degree, something of this kind may still be inlaid; that, though it cannot have that perfect efficacy, as if it had been originally of the piece, yet, if well conducted, it may strengthen the weak parts, and alleviate defects, if not completely remove them."

In conducting my examination of these sentiments, I shall make no remarks upon any particular passages in the book, but consider only the author's general scheme, and the proper and professed object of it. And as the doctor has proposed no particular plan of public education, I shall be as general as he has been, and only show the inconvenience of establishing, by law, any plan of education whatever.

This writer pleads for a plan of education established by the legislature, as the only effectual method of preventing faction in the state, and securing the perpetuity of our excellent constitution, ecclesiastical and civil. I agree with him, in acknowledging the importance of education, as influencing the manners and the conduct of men. I also acknowledge, that an uniform plan of education, agreeable to the principles of any particular form of government, civil or ecclesiastical, would tend to establish and perpetuate that form of government, and prevent civil dissentions and factions in the state. But I should object to the interference of the legislature in this business of education, as prejudicial to the proper design of education, and also to the great ends of civil societies with respect to their present utility. I shall moreover show, that it would be absolutely inconsistent with the true principles of the English government, and could not be carried into execution, to any purpose, without the ruin of our present constitution. I beg the candour of the public, while I endeavour to explain, in as few words as possible, in what manner, I apprehend, this interference of the civil magistrate would operate to obstruct these great ends; and I shall consider these articles separately.

I observed in the first place, that a legal code of education might interfere with the proper design of it. I do not mean what this writer seems to consider as the only object of education, the tranquility of the state, but the forming of wise and virtuous men; which is certainly an object of the greatest importance in every state. If the constitution of a state be a good one, such men will be the greatest bulwarks of it; if it be a bad one, they will be the most able and ready to contribute to its reformation; in either of which cases they will render it the greatest service.

Education is as much an art (founded, as all arts are, upon science) as husbandry, as architecture, or as ship-building. In all these cases we have a practical problem proposed to us, which must be performed by the help of *data* with which experience and observation furnish us. The end of ship-building is to make the best ships, of architecture the best houses, and of education, the best men. Now, of all arts, those stand the fairest chance of being brought to perfection, in which there is opportunity of making the most experiments and trials, and in which there are the greatest number and variety of persons employed in making them. History and experience show, that, *cæteris paribus*, those arts have always, in fact, been brought the soonest, or the nearest to perfection, which have been placed in those favourable circumstances. The reason is, that the operations of the human mind are slow; a number of false hypotheses and conclusions always precede the right one; and in every art, manual or liberal, a number of awkward attempts are made, before we are able to execute any thing which will bear to be shown as a master-piece in its kind; so that to establish the methods and processes of any art, before it have arrived to a state of perfection (of which no man can be a judge) is to fix it in its infancy, to perpetuate every thing that is inconvenient and awkward in it, and to cut off its future growth and improvement. And to establish the methods and processes of any art when it has arrived to perfection is superfluous. It will then recommend and establish itself.

Now I appeal to any person whether any plan of education, which has yet been put in execution in this kingdom, be so perfect as that the establishing of it by authority would not obstruct the great ends of education; or even whether the united genius of man could, at present, form so perfect a plan. Every man who is experienced in the business of education well knows, that the art is in its infancy; but advancing, it is hoped, apace to a state of manhood. In this condition it requires the aid of every circumstance favourable to its natural growth, and dreads nothing so much as being confined and cramped by the unseasonable hand of power. To put it (in its present imperfect state) into the hands of the civil magistrate, in order to fix the mode of it, would be like fixing the dress of a child, and forbidding its clothes ever to be made wider or larger.

Manufacturers and artists of several kinds already complain of the obstruction which is thrown in the way of their arts, by the injudicious acts of former parliaments; and it is the object of our wisest statesmen to get these obstructions removed, by the repeal of those acts. I wish it could not be said, that the business of education is already under too many legal restraints. Let these be removed, and a few more fair experiments made of the different methods of conducting it, before the legislature think proper to interfere any more with it; and by that time, it is hoped, they will see no reason to interfere at all. The business would be conducted to much better purpose, even in favour of their own views, if those views were just and honourable, than it would be under any arbitrary regulations whatever.

To show this scheme of an established method of education in a clearer point of light, let us imagine that what is now proposed had been carried into execution some centuries before this time. For no reason can be assigned for fixing any mode of education at present, which might not have been made use of, with the same appearance of reason, for fixing another approved method a thousand years ago. Suppose Alfred, when he founded the university of Oxford, had made it impossible, that the method of instruction used in his time should ever have been altered. Excellent as that method might have been, for the time in which it was instituted, it would now have been the worst method that is practised in the world. Suppose the number of the arts and sciences, with the manner of teaching them, had been fixed in this kingdom, before the revival of letters and of the arts, it is plain they could never have arrived at their present advanced state among us. We should not have had the honour to lead the way in the most noble discoveries, in the mathematics, philosophy, astronomy, and, I may add, divinity too. And for the same reason, were such an establishment to take place in the present age, it would prevent all great improvements in futurity.

I may add, in this place, that, if we argue from the analogy of education to other arts which are most similar to it, we can never expect to see human nature, about which it is employed, brought to perfection, but in consequence of indulging unbounded liberty, and even caprice in conducting it. The power of nature in producing plants cannot be shown to advantage, but in all possible circumstances of culture. The richest colours, the most fragrant scents, and the most exquisite flavours, which our present gardens and orchards exhibit, would never have been known, if florists and gardeners had been confined in the processes of cultivation; nay if they had not been allowed the utmost licentiousness of fancy in the exercise of their arts. Many of the finest productions of modern gardening have been the result of casual experiment, perhaps of undesigned deviation from established rules. Observations of a similar nature may be made on the methods of breeding cattle, and training animals of all kinds. And why should the rational part of the creation be deprived of that opportunity of diversifying and improving itself, which the vegetable and animal world enjoy?

From new, and seemingly irregular methods of education, perhaps something extraordinary and uncommonly great may spring. At least there would be a fair chance for such productions; and if something odd and eccentric should, now and then, arise from this unbounded liberty of education, the various business of human life may afford proper spheres for such eccentric geniuses.

Education, taken in its most extensive sense, is properly that which *makes the man.* One method of education, therefore, would only produce one kind of men; but the great excellence of human nature consists in the variety of which it is capable. Instead, then, of endeavouring, by uniform and fixed systems of education, to keep mankind always the same, let us give free scope to every thing which may bid fair for introducing more variety among us. The various character of the Athenians was certainly preferable to the uniform character of the Spartans, or to any uniform national character whatever. Is it not universally considered as an advantage to England, that it contains so great a variety of original characters? And is it not, on this account, preferred to France, Spain, or Italy?

Uniformity is the characteristic of the brute creation. Among them every species of birds build their nests with the same materials, and in the same form; the genius and disposition of one individual is that of all; and it is only the education which men give them that raises any of them much above others. But it is the glory of human nature, that the operations of reason, though variable, and by no means infallible, are capable of infinite improvement. We come into the world worse provided than any of the brutes, and for a year or two of our lives, many of them go far beyond us in intellectual accomplishments. But when their faculties are at a full stand, and their enjoyments incapable of variety, or increase, our intellectual powers are growing apace; we are perpetually deriving happiness from new sources, and even before we leave this world are capable of tasting the felicity of angels.

Have we, then, so little sense of the proper excellence of our natures, and of the views of divine providence in our formation, as to catch at a poor advantage adapted to the lower nature of brutes. Rather, let us hold on in the course in which the divine being himself has put us, by giving reason its full play, and throwing off the fetters which shortsighted and ill-judging men have hung upon it. Though, in this course, we be liable to more extravagancies than brutes, governed by blind but unerring instinct, or than men whom mistaken

45

systems of policy have made as uniform in their sentiments and conduct as the brutes, we shall be in the way to attain a degree of perfection and happiness of which they can have no idea.

However, as men are first animals before they can be properly termed rational creatures, and the analogies of individuals extend to societies, a principle something resembling the instinct of animals may, perhaps, suit mankind in their infant state; but then, as we advance in the arts of life, let us, as far as we are able, assert the native freedom of our souls; and, after having been servilely governed like brutes, aspire to the noble privilege of governing ourselves like men.

If it may have been necessary to establish something by law concerning education, that necessity grows less every day, and encourages us to relax the bonds of authority, rather than bind them faster.

Secondly, this scheme of an established mode of education would be prejudicial to the great ends of civil society. The great object of civil society is the happiness of the members of it, in the perfect and undisturbed enjoyment of the more important of our natural rights, for the sake of which, we voluntarily give up others of less consequence to us. But whatever be the blessings of civil society, they may be bought too dear. It is certainly possible to sacrifice too much, at least more than is necessary to be sacrificed for them, in order to produce the greatest sum of happiness in the community. Else why do we complain of tyrannical and oppressive governments? Is it not the meaning of all complaints of this kind, that, in such governments, the subjects are deprived of their most important natural rights, without an equivalent recompense; that all the valuable ends of civil government might be effectually secured, and the members of particular states be much happier upon the whole, if they did not lie under those restrictions.

Now, of all the sources of happiness and enjoyment in human life, the domestic relations are the most constant and copious. With our wives and children we necessarily pass the greatest part of our lives. The connections of friendship are slight in comparison of this intimate domestic union. Views of interest or ambition may divide the nearest friends, but our wives and children are, in general, inseparably connected with us and attached to us. With them all our joys are doubled, and in their affection and assiduity we find consolation under all the troubles and disquietudes of life. For the enjoyments which result from this most delightful intercourse, all mankind, in all ages, have been ready to sacrifice every thing; and for the interruption of this intercourse no compensation whatever can be made by man. What then can be more justly alarming, to a man who has a true taste for happiness, than, either that the choice of his wife, or the education of his children should be under the direction of persons who have no particular knowledge of him, or particular affection for him, and whose views and maxims he might utterly dislike? What prospect of happiness could a man have with such a wife, or such children?

It is possible indeed, that the preservation of some civil societies, such as that of Sparta, may require this sacrifice; but those civil societies must be wretchedly constituted to stand in need of it, and had better be utterly dissolved. Were I a member of such a state, thankful should I be to its governors, if they would permit me peace-ably to retire to any other country, where so great a sacrifice was not required. Indeed, it is hardly possible that a state should require any sacrifice, which I should think of so much importance. And, I doubt not, so many others would be of the same mind, that there would soon be very little reason to complain of the too great increase of commerce in such a country. This, however, would render very necessary another part of our author's scheme; viz. putting a restraint upon travelling abroad, lest too many persons should be willing to leave such a country, and have no inclination to return.

If there be any natural rights which ought not to be sacrificed to the ends of civil society, and no politicians or moralists deny but that there are some (the obligations of religion, for instance, being certainly of a superior nature) it is even more natural to look for these rights among those which respect a man's children, than among those which respect himself; because nature has generally made them dearer to him than himself.

If any trust can be said to be of God, and such as ought not to be relinquished at the command of man, it is that which we have of the education of our children, whom the divine being seems to have put under our immediate care; that we may instruct them in such principles, form them to such manners, and give them such habits of thinking and acting, as we shall judge to be of the greatest importance to their present and future well being.

I believe there is no father in the world (who, to a sense of religion, joins a strong sense of parental affection) who would think his own liberty above half indulged to him, when abridged in so tender a point, as that of providing, to his own satisfaction, for the good conduct and happiness of his offspring. Nature seems to have established such a strong connexion between a parent and his children, at least during the first period of their lives, that to drag them from the asylum of their natural guardians, to force them to public places of education, and to instil into them religious sentiments contrary to the judgement and choice of their parents, would be as cruel as obliging a man to make the greatest personal sacrifice, even that of his conscience, to the civil magistrate.

What part of the persecution which the protestants in France underwent did they complain of more feelingly, and with more justice, than that of their children being forced from them, and carried to be educated in public monasteries? God forbid that the parental affections of free born Britons should ever be put to so severe a trial! or to that which the poor Jews in Portugal suffered; many of whom cut the throats of their children, or threw them into wells, and down precipices, rather than suffer them to be dragged away to be educated under the direction of a popish inquisition; thinking the lives of their children a less sacrifice than that of their principles.

It was a measure similar to that which Dr Brown recommends, at which the whole christian world took the greatest alarm that was ever given to it, in the reign of that great man, but inveterate enemy of christianity, the emperor Julian; who would have shut up the schools of christians, and have forbidden them to teach rhetoric and philosophy. Similar to this scheme, in its nature and tendency, was the most odious measure of the most odious ministry that ever sat at the helm of the British government, and which was providentially defeated the very day that it was to have been carried into execution; I mean the SCHISM BILL, patronized by the Tory ministers in the latter end of the reign of queen Ann:[15] Should these measures be resumed, and pursued, Farewell, a long farewell to England's greatness! Nor would this be said in a hasty fit of unreasonable despair. For, besides that such a measure as this could not but have many extensive consequences; it is not to be doubted, but that whoever they be who do thus much, they both *can* and *will* do more. Such a scheme as this will never be pushed for its own sake only.

In examining the present operation and utility of any scheme of

[15] The Schism Act (1714) was the culmination of a series of legislative attempts by the Tories to shut dissenting academies and begin the curtailment of legal toleration.

policy, we ought to take into consideration the ease or the difficulty of carrying it into execution. For if the disturbance, which would be occasioned by bringing it into execution, would be so great an inconvenience, as to overbalance the good to be effected by it, it were better never to attempt it. Now, though the doctor hath laid down no particular scheme of public and established education, and therefore we cannot judge of the particular difficulties which would attend the establishing of it; yet, if it be such as would answer the end proposed by him, this difficulty would appear to me absolutely insuperable, in such a country as England.

Whatever be the *religious, moral, and political principles*, which are thought conducive to the good of the society, if they must be *effectually instilled into the infant and growing minds of the community*, it can never be done without taking the children very early from their parents, and cutting off all communication with them, till they be arrived to maturity, and their judgments be absolutely fixed. And if this author judged, that the reason why a scheme of this nature did not take place in Athens, was the difficulty of establishing it, after the people were tolerably civilized; he must certainly judge it to be infinitely more difficult, among a people so much farther advanced in the arts of life than the Athenians.

He well observed, p. 53, that, "to give children a public education where no education had taken place, was natural and practicable;" but he seems to be aware, that an attempt to carry any such plan into execution, in the most flourishing period of a free and civilized state, would be highly unnatural, without the least probable hope of success, and dangerous to such as took it in hand. For he says, p. 52, that, "to effect a change of government only is a work sufficient for the abilities of the greatest legislator; but to overturn all the preestablished habits of the head and heart, to destroy or reverse all the fixed associations, maxims, manners, and principles, were a labour which might well be ranked among the most extravagant legends of fabulous Greece."

What might be expected from the business of education being lodged by the state in the hands of any one set of men, may be imagined from the alarm which the Newtonian system gave to all philosophers at the time of its first publication; and from what passed at Oxford with respect to Locke's *Essay on the human understanding*, which hath done so much honour to the English nation in the eyes of all the learned world. We are told by the authors of *Biographia Britan-*

nica,[16] in the life of Mr Locke, that "there was a meeting of the heads of houses at Oxford, where it was proposed to censure, and discourage the reading of this Essay; and that, after various debates, it was concluded, that, without any public censure, each head of a house shall endeavour to prevent its being read in his own college." This passed but a little before Mr Locke's death, and about fourteen years after the first publication of the Essay.

Hitherto I have argued against established modes of education upon general principles, showing how unfavourable they are to the great ends of civil society, with only occasional references to the English constitution; and in these arguments I have, likewise, supposed these methods of education, whatever they be, actually established, and to have operated to their full extent. I shall now add, that, before these methods can be established, and produce their full effect, they must occasion a very considerable alteration in the English constitution, and almost inevitably destroy the freedom of it; so that the thing which would, in fact, be perpetuated, would not be the present constitution of England, but something very different from it, and more despotic. An alteration of so great importance, which tends to defeat one of the principal objects of this government, cannot but give just cause of alarm to every friend of the present happy constitution and liberties of this country. In support of this assertion, I desire no other argument than that with which Dr Brown himself furnishes me, from the influence he allows to education, operating, likewise, in the very manner which he describes, and to the very end for which he advises the establishing of its mode.

Education is considered by the doctor only in a political view, as useful to instil into the minds of youth particular maxims of policy, and to give them an attachment to particular forms of it; or as tending to superinduce such habits of mind, and to give such a general turn of thinking, as would correspond with the genius of a particular state. This education he would have to be universal and uniform; and indeed, if it were not so, it could not possibly answer the end proposed. It must, therefore, be conducted by *one set of men*. But it is impossible to find any set of men, who shall have an equal regard to all the parts of our constitution; and whatever part is neglected in such a system of education, it cannot fail to be a sufferer.

[16] *Biographia Britannica*, 6 vols. (London, 1747–66).

The English government is a mixture of regal, aristocratical, and democratical power; and if the public education should be more favourable to any one of these than to another, or more than its present importance in the constitution requires, the balance of the whole would necessarily be lost. Too much weight would be thrown into some of the scales, and the constitution be overturned. If the Commons, representing the body of the people, had the choice of these public instructors, which is almost impossible, we should see a republic rise out of the ruins of our present government; if the Lords, which is highly improbable, we should, in the end, have an aristocracy; and if the court had this nomination, which it may be taken for granted would be the case (as all the executive power of the state is already lodged in the hands of the sovereign) it could not but occasion a very dangerous accession of power to the crown; and we might justly expect a system of education, principles, and manners favourable to despotism. Every man would be educated with principles, which would lead him to concur with the views of the court. All that opposition from the country, which is so salutary in this nation, and so essential to the liberties of England, would be at an end. And when once the *spirit* of despotism was thus established, and had triumphed over all opposition, we might soon expect to see the *forms* of it established too, and thereby the very doors shut against old English liberty, and effectually guarded against the possibility of its return, except by violence; which would then be the only method of its re-entrance.

It is evident to common understanding, that the true spirit and maxims of a mixed government can no otherwise be continued, than by every man's educating his children in his own way; and that if any one part provided for the education of the whole, that part would soon gain the ascendancy; and, if it were capable of it, would become the whole. Were a state, for instance, to consist of papists and protestants, and the papists to have the sole power of education, protestantism would expire with that generation: whereas, if the papists and protestants educated each their own children, the same proportion would continue to subsist between them, and the balance of power would remain the same. For the same reason the only method of preserving the balance, which at present subsists among the several political and religious parties in Great-Britain, is for each to provide for the education of their own children.

In this way, there will be a fair prospect of things continuing nearly upon their present footing, for a considerable time; but subject to those gradual alterations which, it may be hoped, will prove favourable to the best interests of the society upon the whole. Whereas, were the direction of the whole business of education thrown into the hands of the court, it would be such an accession of power to the regal part of our constitution, as could not fail to alarm all the friends of civil liberty; as all the friends of religious liberty would be justly alarmed, if it should devolve upon the established clergy. And it were the greatest injustice to the good sense of free born Britons, to suppose the noble spirit of religious liberty, and a zeal for the rights of free inquiry confined within the narrow circle of Protestant Dissenters.

Considering the whole of what hath been advanced in this section, I think it sufficiently appears, that education is a branch of civil liberty, which ought by no means to be surrendered into the hands of the magistrate; and that the best interests of society require, that the right of conducting it should be inviolably preserved to individuals.

SECTION V.

Of Religious Liberty, and Toleration in general.

The most important question concerning the extent of civil government is, whether the civil magistrate ought to extend his authority to matters of *religion*; and the only method of deciding this important question, as it appears to me, is to have recourse at once to first principles, and the ultimate rule concerning every thing that respects a society; viz. whether such interference of the civil magistrate appear to be for the public good. And as all arguments *a priori*, in matters of policy, are apt to be fallacious, *fact* and *experience* seem to be our only safe guides. Now these, as far as our knowledge of history extends, declare clearly for no interference in this case at all, or, at least, for as little as is possible. Those societies have ever enjoyed the most happiness, and have been, *cæteris paribus*, in the most flourishing state, where the civil magistrates have meddled the least with religion, and where they have the most closely confined their attention to what immediately affects the civil interests of their fellow citizens.

Civil and religious matters (taking the words in their usual acceptation) seem to be so distinct, that it can only be in very uncommon emergencies, where, for instance, religious quarrels among the members of the state rise very high, that the civil magistrate can have any call, or pretence, for interfering with religion.

[It is, indeed, impossible to name any two things, about which men are concerned, so remote in their nature, but that they have some connections and mutual influences; but were I asked what two things I should think to be in the *least danger* of being confounded, and which even the ingenuity of man could find the *least pretence* for involving together, I should say the things that relate to *this life*, and those that relate to the *life to come*. Defining the object of civil government, in the most extensive sense, to be the making provision for the secure and comfortable enjoyment of this life, by preventing one man from injuring another in his person or property; I should think the office of the civil magistrate to be in no great danger of being incroached upon, by the methods that men might think proper to take, to provide for their happiness after death.

All the civil societies we enter into in this life will be dissolved by death. When this life is over, I shall not be able to claim any of the privileges of an Englishman; I shall not be bound by any of the laws of England, nor shall I owe any allegiance to its sovereign. When, therefore, my situation in a future life shall have no connection with my privileges or obligations as an Englishman, why should those persons who make laws for Englishmen interfere with my conduct, with respect to a state, to which their power does not extend. Besides, we know that infinite mischiefs have arisen from this interference of government in the business of religion; and we have yet seen no inconvenience to have arisen from the want, or the relaxation of it.]

The fine country of Flanders, the most flourishing and opulent then in Europe, was absolutely ruined, past recovery, by the mad attempt of Philip the second, to introduce the popish inquisition into that country. France was greatly hurt by the revocation of the edict of Nantz[17] whereas England was a great gainer on both occasions, by granting an asylum for those persecuted industrious people; who repaid us for our kindness, by the introduction of many useful arts and manufactures, which were the foundation of our present commerce, riches, and power.

Pensylvania flourished much more than New England, or than any other of the English settlements in North America, evidently in consequence of giving more liberty in matters of religion, at its first establishment. Holland has found its advantage in the indulgence she gives to a great variety of religious persuasions. England has also been much more flourishing and happy, since the *establishment*, as it may properly enough be stiled, of the dissenting method of worship, by what is commonly called the *act of toleration*. And all the sensible part of Europe concur in thinking, both that the Polish dissidents have a right to all the privileges of other Polish citizens; and that it would be much happier for that country if their claims were quietly admitted; and none but interested bigots opposed their demands.

If we look a little farther off from home, let it be said, what inconvenience did Jenghis khan, Tamerlane, and other eastern conquerors ever find from leaving religion to its natural course in the countries they subdued, and from having christians, mahometans, and a variety of pagans under the same form of civil government? Are not both christianity and mohammedanism, in fact, established (the former at least fully tolerated) in Turkey; and what inconvenience, worth mentioning, has ever arisen from it?

Pity it is then, that more and fairer experiments are not made; when, judging from what is past, the consequences of *unbounded liberty, in matters of religion*, promise to be so very favourable to the best interests of mankind.

I am aware, that the connexion between civil and religious affairs, will be urged for the necessity of some interference of the legislature with religion; and, as I observed before, I do not deny the connection. But as this connection has always been found to be the greatest in barbarous nations, and imperfect governments, to which it lends an useful aid; it may be presumed, that it is gradually growing less

---

[17] 'The Edict of Nantes' (1685).

necessary; and that, in the present advanced state of human society, there is very little occasion for it. For my own part, I have no apprehension, but that, at this day, the laws might be obeyed very well without any ecclesiastical sanctions, enforced by the civil magistrate.

Not that I think religion will ever be a matter of indifference in civil society: that is impossible, if the word be understood in its greatest latitude, and by religion we mean that principle whereby men are influenced by the dread of evil, or the hope of reward from any unknown and invisible causes, whether the good or evil be expected to take place in this world or another; comprehending enthusiasm, superstition, and every species of false religion, as well as the true. Nor is such an event at all desirable; nay, the more just motives men have to the same good actions, the better; but religious motives may still operate in favour of the civil laws, without such a connection as has been formed between them in ecclesiastical establishments; and, I think, this end would be answered even better without that connection.

In all the modes of religion, which subsist among mankind, however subversive of virtue they may be in theory, there is some *salvo* for good morals; so that, in fact, they enforce the more essential parts, at least, of that conduct, which the good order of society requires. Besides, it might be expected, that if all the modes of religion were equally protected by the civil magistrate, they would all vie with one another, which should best deserve that protection. This, however, is, in fact, all the alliance that can take place between religion and civil policy, each enforcing the same conduct by different motives. Any other *alliance between church and state* is only the alliance of different sorts of worldly minded men, for their temporal emolument.

If I be urged with the horrid excesses of the anabaptists in Germany, about the time of the reformation; of the Levellers in England, during the civil wars; and the shocking practices of that people in Asia, from whom we borrow the term *assassin*; I answer, that, besides its being absolutely chimerical to apprehend any such extravagances at present, and that they can never subsist long; such outrages as these, against the peace of society, may be restrained by the civil magistrate, without his troubling himself about religious opinions. If a man commit murder, let him be punished as a murderer, and let no regard be paid to his plea of conscience for committing the action; but let not the opinions, which led to the action be meddled with: for then, it is probable, that more harm will be done than good, and, that for a small evident advantage, risk will be run of endless and unknown evils; or if the civil magistrate never interfere in religion but in such cases as those before mentioned, the friends of liberty will have no great reason to complain. Considering what great encroachments have been made upon their rights in several countries of Europe, they will be satisfied if *part of the load* be removed. They will support themselves with the hope, that, as the state will certainly find a solid advantage in every relaxation of its claim upon men's consciences, it will relax more and more of its pretended rights; till, at last, religious opinions, and religious actions, be as free as the air we breathe, or the light of the common sun.

I acknowledge, with the statesman, that the proper object of the civil magistrate is the peace and well being of society, and that whatever tends to disturb that peace and well being, properly comes under his cognisance. I acknowledge several religious and moral, as well as political principles have a near connection with the well being of society. But, as was more fully explained before, there are many cases, in which the happiness of society is nearly concerned, in which it would, nevertheless, be the greatest impropriety for the civil magistrate to interfere; as in many of the duties of private life, the obligations of gratitude, &c. In all such cases, where the well being of society is most nearly concerned, the civil magistrate has no right to interfere, unless he can do it to good purpose. There is no difference, I apprehend, to be made in this case, between the *right*, and the *wisdom* of interference. If the interference would be for the good of the society upon the whole, it is wise, and right; if it would do more harm than good, it is foolish and wrong. Let the sagacious statesman, therefore, consider, whether the interference of the civil magistrate be, in its own nature, calculated to prevent the violation of the religious and moral principles he may wish to enforce. I think it is clear, that when they are in danger of being violated, his presence is so far from tending to remedy the evil, that it must necessarily inflame it, and make it worse.

It is universally understood, that REASON and AUTHORITY are two things, and that they have generally been opposed to one another.[18] The hand of power, therefore, on the side of any set of

---

[18] In his essay 'Of the Origin of Government' Hume had described a similar conflict between 'Authority and Liberty'.

principles cannot but be a suspicious circumstance. And though the injunction of the magistrate may silence *voices*, it multiplies *whispers*; and those whispers are the things at which he has the most reason to be alarmed.

Besides, it is universally true, that where the civil magistrate has the greatest pretence for interfering in religious and moral principles, his interference (supposing there were no impropriety in it) is the least necessary. If the opinions and principles in question, be evidently subversive of all religion and all civil society, they must be evidently false, and easy to refute; so that there can be no danger of their spreading; and the patrons of them may safely be suffered to maintain them in the most open manner they choose.

To mention those religious and moral principles which Dr Brown produces, as the most destructive to the well being of society; namely, that *there is no God*, and that *there is no faith to be kept with heretics*. So far am I from being of his opinion, that it is necessary to guard against these principles by severe penalties, and not to tolerate those who maintain them, that I think, of all opinions, surely such as these have nothing formidable or alarming in them. They can have no terrors but what the magistrate himself, by his ill-judged opposition, may give them. Persecution may procure friends to any cause, and possibly to this, but hardly any thing else can do it. It is unquestionable, that there are more atheists and infidels of all kinds in Spain and Italy, where religion is so well guarded, than in England; and it is, perhaps, principally owing to the laws in favour of christianity, that there are so many deists in this country.

For my own part, I cannot help thinking the principles of Dr Brown very dangerous in a free state, and therefore cannot but wish they were exterminated. But I should not think that silencing him would be the best method of doing it. No, let him, by all means, be encouraged in making his sentiments public; both that their dangerous tendency, and their futility may more clearly appear. Had I the direction of the press, he should be welcome to my *imprimatur* for any thing he should please to favour the world with; and ready, if I know myself, should I be, to furnish him with every convenience in my power for that purpose. It is for the interest of truth that every thing be viewed in fair and open day light, and it can only be some sinister purpose that is favoured by darkness or concealment of any kind. My sentiments may be fallacious, but if no body were allowed to write against me, how could that fallacy be made to appear? Be the prayer of the magnanimous Ajax ever mine,

Ποιησον δ' αυϑ̓ζην, δος δ' οφϑαλμοισιν ιδεσϑαι.
Εν δε φαει ται ολεσσον

Homer. Lib. 17. v. 646.[19]

This writer artfully mentions only three opinions or principles, one under each class of *religion, morals,* and *politics,* as necessary to be guarded by civil penalties, and not to be tolerated; and, no doubt, he has chosen those principles which a friend to his country would most wish to have suppressed, and with regard to which, he would least scrupulously examine the means that might be used to suppress them. This, Britons, is the method in which arbitrary power has ever been introduced; and is well known to have been the method used by the thirty tyrants of Athens. They first cut off persons the most generally obnoxious, and such as the standing laws could not reach; and even that intelligent people were so far duped by their resentment, that they were not aware, that the very same methods might be employed to take off the worthiest men in the city. And if ever arbitrary power should gain ground in England, it will be by means of the seeming necessity of having recourse to illegal methods, in order to come at opinions or persons generally obnoxious. But when these illegal practices have once been authorized, and have passed into precedents, all persons, and all opinions will lie at the mercy of the prime minister, who will animadvert upon whatever gives him umbrage.

Happy would it be for the unsuspecting sons of liberty, if their enemies would say, at first, how far they meant to proceed against them. To say, as Dr Brown does, that there are *many* opinions and principles which ought not to be tolerated, and to instance only in *three,* is very suspicious and alarming. Let him say, in the name of all the friends of liberty, I challenge him, or any of his friends to say, how many more he has thought proper not to mention, and what they are; that we may not admit the foot of arbitrary power, before we see what size of a body the monster has to follow it.

Such is the connection and gradation of opinions, that if once we admit there are *some* which ought to be guarded by civil penalties, it will ever be impossible to distinguish, to general satisfaction, between those which may be tolerated, and those which may not. No two men

---

[19] 'Father Zeus, deliver thou from the darkness the sons of the Achaeans, and make clear sky, and grant us to see with our eyes.' *Iliad*, XVII.646 (translated by A. T. Murray, Loeb 1917).

living, were they questioned strictly, would give the same list of such fundamentals. Far easier were it to distinguish the exact boundaries of the animal, vegetable, and mineral kingdoms in nature, which yet naturalists find to be impossible. But a happy circumstance it is for human society, that, in religion and morals, there is no necessity to distinguish them at all. The more important will guard themselves by their own evidence, and the less important do not deserve to be guarded.

Political principles, indeed, may require penal sanctions; but then it is for the very same reason that religious and moral principles require none. It is because they do not carry their own evidence along with them. Governments actually established must guard themselves by penalties and intolerance, because forms of government, and persons presiding in them, being nearly arbitrary, it may not be very evident that a different government, or different governors, would not be better for a state. Laws relating to treason are to be considered as arising from the principle of self-preservation. But even with respect to civil government, it is better not to guard every thing so strongly as that no alteration can ever be made in it. Nay, alterations are daily proposed, and daily take place in our civil government, in things both of great and small consequence. They are improvements in religion only that receive no countenance from the state: a fate singular and hard!

Besides, so many are the subtle distinctions relating to religion and morals, that no magistrate or body of magistrates, could be supposed to enter into them; and yet, without entering into them, no laws they could make would be effectual. To instance in the first of Dr Brown's principles, and the most essential of them, viz. the being of a God. The magistrate must define strictly what he means by the term God, for otherwise Epicureans and Spinozists might be no atheists; or Arians or Athanasians might be obnoxious to the law. The magistrate must likewise punish, not only those who directly maintain the principles of Atheism (for evasions are so easy to find, that such laws would hurt no body) but he must punish those who do it indirectly; and what opinions are there not, in religion, morals, and even natural philosophy, which might not be said to *lead to* Atheism? The doctrine of equivocal generation, for instance, might certainly be thought of this kind, as well as many others, which have been very harmlessly maintained by many good christians.

I am sensible, that in the few particulars which Dr Brown has

59

thought proper to mention, his intolerant principles are countenanced by Mr Locke; but, as far as I can recollect, these are all the opinions which he would not tolerate; whereas this writer asserts there are *many*; so that he must provide himself with some other authority for the rest. Besides I make no doubt, the great Mr Locke would, without the least reluctance, have given up any of his assertions, upon finding so bad an use made of them, and that the consequences of them were so very unfavourable to his own great object, and contradictory to his leading principles; and that he would, with indignation, have given up any adherents to arbitrary power, who, from such a pretence as this, should have claimed his protection from the generous pursuit of the friends of liberty, of reason, and of mankind. After all, the controversy is not about men, but principles. And so great an enemy as Mr Locke, to all authority in matters of opinion, would not have been so inconsistent as to have excepted his own.

It will be said, that a regard to liberty itself must plead for one exception to the principles of toleration. The papists, it is alleged, are such determined enemies to liberty, civil and ecclesiastical, and so effectually alienated from the interests of a protestant country and government, that protestants, who have a regard for their own safety, and the great cause in which they are engaged, cannot tolerate them. If they do it, it is at their own peril; so that the persecution of papists is, in fact, nothing more than a dictate of self-preservation.

This plea, I own, is plausible; and two centuries ago it is no wonder it had considerable weight; but persecution by *protestants*, in this enlightened age, appears so utterly repugnant to the great principle of their cause, that I wish they would view it in every point of light, before they seriously adopt any such measure. And I cannot help thinking, that the result of a more mature consideration of this subject will not be to *render evil for evil* to our old mother church, but rather a more indulgent treatment than we have as yet vouchsafed to afford her.

In the first place, I cannot imagine that the increase of popery, in these kingdoms, will ever be so considerable, as to give any just alarm to the friends of liberty. All the address and assiduity of man cannot, certainly, recommend so absurd a system of faith and practice to any but the lowest and most illiterate of our common people, who can never have any degree of influence in the state. The number of popish gentry must grow less; partly through the influence of fashion, and partly through the conviction of those who have a liberal education, which will necessarily throw protestant books into their hands.

The French translator of Warburton's *Alliance*, in an address to Cardinal Fleury, (in which he recommends such a system of church establishment and toleration as this of the Bishop of Gloucester) observes, that the number of Roman catholics in England diminishes every day, and that the only reason why they are not so good subjects in this country, as they are in Holland, is, that they are under more restraints here.

If the popish priests and missionaries have the success which it is pretended they have, I am almost persuaded, that the most effectual arguments they have employed for this purpose, have been drawn from the rigour of our present laws respecting the papists. They tell the people, that, conscious of the weakness of our cause, we dare not give them full liberty to teach and exercise their religion; knowing that the excellency of it is such, that, if it were publicly exhibited, it would attract universal admiration; and that what we are not able to silence by argument, we suppress by force.

Besides, the traces and remains of popery are so striking in the book of common prayer, and in the whole of our ecclesiastical establishment, that the derivation of it from the popish system cannot be concealed; and hence it may not be difficult for an artful papist, to persuade many of the common people to quit the shadow, and have recourse to the substance; to abandon the interests of an apostate child, and adopt that of its ancient and venerable parent.

Let the church of England then, before it be too late, make a farther reformation from popery, and leave fewer of the symbols of the Romish church about her; and the ideas of her members being more remote from every thing that has any connection with popery, and popish missionaries will have much more difficulty in making them comprehend and relish it. A convert to popery from any of the sects of protestant dissenters (who are farther removed from the popish system than the church of England) is very rarely heard of. And this effect is not owing to any particular care of their ministers to guard their hearers against popery; but because the whole system of their faith and practice is so contrary to it, that even the common people among them, would as soon turn mahometans, or pagans, as become papists.

Instead, then, of using more rigour with the papists, let us allow them a full toleration. We should, at least, by this means, be better judges of their number, and increase. And I also think they would be much less formidable in these circumstances, than they are at present. If they be enemies, an open enemy is less dangerous than a secret one. And if our ecclesiastical establishment must not be reformed, and removed farther from popery; let the clergy, as the best *succedaneum* for such an effectual antidote against their poison, show more zeal in the discharge of their parochial duties, and give more attention to their flocks. Half the zeal which the papists employ, to make converts, would be more than sufficient to prevent any from being made. Whose business is it to counteract the endeavours of the popish emissaries, but those whom the state has appointed the guardians of the people in spiritual matters; and what is their calling in the aid of the civil power, but an acknowledgement of a neglect of their proper duty?

It may be said, that the particular situation of this country should be a motive with all the friends of our happy constitution, to keep a watchful eye over the papists; since a popish religion may, at length, fix a popish pretender upon the throne of these kingdoms. Seriously as this argument for persecution might have been urged formerly, I cannot help thinking that, ever since the last rebellion, the apprehension on which it is grounded, is become absolutely chimerical, and therefore that it does not deserve a serious answer. After the pope himself has refused to acknowledge the heir of the Stuart family to be king of England, what can a papist, as such, have to plead for him? And, for my own part, I make no doubt, there are men of good sense among the popish gentry, at least, and persons of property of that persuasion, as well as among persons of other religious professions; and therefore, that if they lay under fewer civil disadvantages, they would not only cheerfully acquiesce in, but would become zealously attached to our excellent form of *free government*; and that, upon any emergency, they would bravely stand up for it, protestant as it is, in opposition to any popish system of *arbitrary power* whatever.

Besides, when a popish country is at this very time,* showing us an example of a toleration, more perfect, in several respects, than any which the church of England allows to those who dissent from her, is it not time to advance a little farther?[20] Political considerations may

*Written in 1768.

[20] The condition of Orthodox and Reformed 'dissidents' in a Poland re-catholicized in the seventeenth century had been a source of considerable tension. A series of 'constitu-

justly be allowed to have some weight in this case. France may reasonably be expected to follow, and improve upon the example of Poland; and if we do not make some speedy improvement of liberty, that great and indefatigable rival power, by one master stroke of policy, may almost depopulate this great and flourishing kingdom.

We often hear it said, that if France grows wise, and admits of toleration, England is undone. Novelty, and a milder climate, will, no doubt, attract multitudes; and whenever the French make a reformation, as their minds are much more enlightened, than those of the English reformers were, when our present establishment was fixed, their reformation will, in all probability, be much more perfect than ours. And if the French through our folly, and the ambition, avarice, or baseness of some spiritual dignitaries, should be permitted to take the lead in this noble work, and our emulation be not roused by their example, the future motto of England may, with too much propriety, be taken from Bacon's speaking statue, TIME IS PAST.

SECTION VI.

Some distinctions that have been made on the subject of religious liberty, and toleration considered.

In order to illustrate some of the fundamental principles of religious liberty, I beg the reader's indulgence while I animadvert on a few distinctions that have been suggested by some persons who have written, at different times, on this subject, and which I think have tended to introduce confusion into our ideas concerning it. Many of

tions' imperilling the legal equality and rights of these 'dissidents' and their worship were reversed in October and November 1767, though only with the armed intervention of the Russians. See the fascinating discussion in the preface and in Chapter IV of the *Annual Register . . . for the Year 1767.*

my readers may think some of the cases I shall mention, unworthy of the notice I have taken of them, but I hope they will excuse my giving them a place in this section, when they consider that it is, at least, possible they may have occasioned some difficulty to other persons, unused to these speculations.

I. Religion is sometimes considered as of *a personal*, and sometimes as of *a political* nature. In some measure, indeed, every thing that concerns individuals must affect the societies which they compose; but it by no means follows, that it is, therefore, *right*, or *wise* for societies (*i.e.* mankind collectively taken) to intermeddle with every thing, so as to make laws, and appoint sanctions concerning every thing; because, in numberless cases, more confusion and inconvenience would necessarily arise from the interference, than from the want of it; since individuals are, in many respects, better situated for the purpose of judging and providing for themselves than magistrates, as such, can be.

These, and many other reasons, lead me to consider the business of religion, and every thing fairly connected with it, as intirely *a personal concern*, and altogether foreign to the nature, object, and use of civil magistracy.

Besides, there is something in the nature of religion that makes it more than *out of the proper sphere*, or province of the civil magistrate to intermeddle with it. The duties of religion, properly understood, seem to be, in some measure, incompatible with the interference of the civil power. For the purpose and object of religion necessarily suppose *the powers of individuals*, and a *responsibility*, which is the consequence of those powers; so that the civil magistrate, by taking any of those powers from individuals, and assuming them to himself, doth so far incapacitate them for the duties of religion. If, for instance, I be commanded by divine authority to *search for scriptures*, and the magistrate forbid me the use of them, how can I discharge my duty? And for the same reason, I must think the authority of the magistrates opposed to that of God, in every case in which human laws impede the use of my faculties in matters of religion.

As a being capable of immortal life (which is a thing of infinitely more consequence to me than all the political considerations of this world) I must endeavour to render myself acceptable to God, by such dispositions and such conduct, as he has required, in order to fit me for future happiness. For this purpose, it is evidently requisite, that I diligently use my reason, in order to make myself acquainted with the will of God; and also that I have liberty to do whatever I believe he requires, provided I do not molest my fellow creatures by such assumed liberty. But all human establishments, as such, obstruct freedom of inquiry in matters of religion, by laying an *undue bias* upon the mind, if they be not such, as by their express constitutions prevent all inquiry, and preclude every possible effect of it.

Christianity, by being a more spiritual and moral constitution than any other form of religion that ever appeared in the world, requires men to think and act for themselves more accurately than any other. But human establishments, by calling off men's attention from the commandments of God to those of men, tend to defeat the great ends of religion. They are, therefore, incompatible with the genius of christianity.

II. In examining the right of the civil magistrate to establish any mode of religion, or that of the subject to oppose it, the *goodness* of the religion, or of the mode of it, is not to be taken into the question; but only the *propriety* (which is the same with the *utility*) of the civil magistrates as such, interfering in the business. For what the magistrate may think to be very just, and even conducive to the good of society, the subject may think to be wrong, and hurtful to it. If a christian magistrate hath a right to establish any mode of the christian religion, or the christian religion in general, a Mahometan governor must have the same right to establish the Mahometan religion; and no liberty can be claimed by a christian under a Mahometan government, to exercise the christian religion, that may not, in the same degree, be claimed by a Mahometan subject of a christian government, to exercise the Mahometan religion. Also, if it be unreasonable and oppressive to oblige christian subjects to support the Mahometan religion, it is equally unreasonable and oppressive to oblige a Mahometan to support the christian religion, in the place where he resides; or to oblige christians of one denomination to support another mode of it, which they do not approve.

The authority of God and conscience may always, with equal justice, be opposed to human authority; and the appeal of Peter and John to the Jewish magistrates, concerning their obligation to *obey God rather than man*, will equally serve a Protestant in a Popish establishment, or a Dissenter of any kind in a Protestant one. It is of no avail to the Papist, or the Protestant, in any establishment, to pretend that the religion they enforce is *true*, or that it is the same, in general, with that which those who dissent from them profess; because the Protestant and the Dissenter do not object to the establishment in those respects in which they believe it to be *true*, but in those in which they believe it to be *false*, and to require them to believe and do what their conscience disapproves. And for a Protestant of any denomination whatever, to maintain his own right to resist the impositions of a Popish government, and at the same time to insist upon a right to impose upon his fellow christians of other Protestant denominations, is too absurd to admit of a formal refutation.

III. Some persons, of narrow minds, may be ready to admit of a plea for the toleration of all sects of *Protestants*. They may bear them some degree of good will, as *brethren*, or at least, as *distant relations*, though the blood in their veins be not equally pure with their own; but, in order to demonstrate that there may be a licentiousness in toleration, and that we must stop somewhere, they say, "What must we do with *heathens* and *atheists*." I answer, the very same that you, christians, would wish that heathens and atheists, in your situation, should do to you, being in theirs. If your party has been so long in power, that you cannot, even in supposition, separate the idea of it from that of the authority which has been so long connected with it; read the history of the primitive church, and see what it was that the first christians wished and pleaded for, under the Pagan emperors. Read the ancient christian apologies; and do the infidels of the present age the justice to put them, or at least part of them, into their mouths.

IV. Others have the moderation and good sense to admit the reasonableness of persons being allowed to judge for themselves, and to *think* as they please in matters of religion, and even to exercise whatever mode of religion their consciences approve of; but they will not admit of any thing that has a tendency to increase the obnoxious sect; no publication of books, or other attempts to make proselytes; not even a reflection upon the established religion, though it be necessary to a vindication of their own. But what signifies a privilege of judging for ourselves, if we have not the necessary means of forming a right judgement, by the perusal of books containing the evidence of both sides of the question? What some distinguish by the names of *active* and *passive* opposition to an established religion, differ only in name and degree. To defend myself, and to attack my adversary, is, in many cases, the very same thing, and the one cannot be done without the other.

Besides, the persons who make use of this distinction, should consider that, for the reasons they allege, the Jewish rulers did right to forbid Peter and John to preach, or to teach, in the name of Jesus of Nazareth, and that Peter and John did wrong in not submitting to that prohibition. They should consider that the primitive christians, under heathen governments, had no right, according to their maxims, to any thing more than the private exercise of their worship, and that they offended against *the powers that then were*, and that were *ordained of God*,[21] when they wrote the excellent books, and took the pains they did to propagate their religion among all ranks of men, and among all nations of the world; though they acted in obedience to the solemn injunction of our Lord, who bade them *go and preach the gospel to every creature*.[22]

By *the gospel* every christian will, and must understand, the gospel in its purity; *i.e.* what he apprehends to be the pure gospel; in opposition, not only to heathenism, and religions *fundamentally false*, but to erroneous christianity, or to religions that are *in part true*. Whatever be the religious opinions, therefore, that I seriously think are agreeable to the word of God, and of importance to the happiness of mankind, I look upon myself as obliged to take every prudent method of propagating them, both by the use of speech and writing; and the man who refrains from doing this, when he is convinced that he should do good upon the whole by attempting it, whatever risk he might run in consequence of opposing anti-christian establishments, is a traitor to his proper lord and master, and shows that he fears more *them who can only kill the body* (whether by the heathen methods of beheading, crucifying, throwing to the wild beasts, &c. or the christian methods of burning alive, and roasting before a slow fire) than him, *who can cast both soul and body into hell*.[23]

V. It is said by some, who think themselves obliged to vindicate the conduct of Christ and his apostles, that, though no *general* plea to oppose an established religion can be admitted, in excuse of a pretended reformer, yet that a *special* plea, such as a belief of a divine commission, will excuse him. But I can see no material difference in these cases. The voice of *conscience* is, in all cases, as the *voice of God* to

---

[21] Romans 13: 1–2.   [22] Mark 16: 15.   [23] Matthew 10: 28.

every man. It is, therefore, my duty to endeavour to enlighten the minds of my friends, my countrymen, and mankind in general, as far as I have ability and opportunity; and to exert myself with more or less zeal, in proportion, as I myself shall judge the importance of the occasion requires; let my honest endeavours be considered as ever so factious and seditious, by those who are aggrieved by them. It is no new cry among the enemies of reformation, *The men who have turned the world upside down are come hither also.*[24]

VI. There are some who confine the obligation to propagate christianity to the *clergy*, and even to those of them who have a *regular commission* for that purpose, according to the form of established churches; and say that *laymen* cannot be under any obligation ˎto trouble themselves about it, in whatever part of the world they be cast; and what they say concerning the propagation of christianity they would extend to the reformation of it. But I can see no foundation for this distinction, either in reason, or in the scriptures. The propagation, or reformation of christianity, is comprehended in the general idea of *promoting useful knowledge* of any kind, and this is certainly the duty of every man, in proportion to his ability and opportunity.

Our Saviour gives no hint of any difference between *clergy* and *laity* among his disciples. The twelve apostles were only distinguished by him as appointed witnesses of his life, death, and resurrection. After the descent of the Holy Ghost, supernatural gifts were equally communicated to all christian converts. The distinction of *elders* was only such as years and experience intitled men to, and only respected the internal government of particular churches. As to the propagation of christianity abroad, or the reformation of corruptions in it at home, there is nothing in the scriptures, that can lead us to imagine it to be the duty of one man more than another. Every man who understands the christian religion, I consider as having the same commission to teach it, as that of any bishop, in England, or in Rome.

VII. Some of the advocates for establishments lay great stress on the distinction between *positive* and *negative* restraints put upon dissenters. The former they affect to disclaim, but the latter they avow, and pretend that it is no persecution. But here I can find no real difference, except in degree. An exclusion from an advantage, and a subjection to a positive disadvantage agree in this, that a man who is

---

[24] Acts 17: 6.

subject to either of them is in *a worse condition* on that account, than he would otherwise have been. If a man, for conscience sake, be excluded from a lucrative office, to which another person, of a different persuasion, has access; he suffers as much, as if the office had been open to him, and a fine, equal to the advantage he would have gained by it, imposed upon him. Nay, it is easy to suppose cases, in which negative restraints may be a greater hardship than positive ones. The *interdiction of fire and water* is not a sentence of positive punishment, and yet banishment, or death must be the consequence. Notwithstanding all this, negative restraints, however severe, must not be called persecution, while positive restraints, how light soever, cannot be denied to fall under that obnoxious appellation.

In reality those who defend the necessity and propriety of laying dissenters under negative restraints, without choosing to be advocates for positive ones, are only afraid of the term *persecution*, which, happily for the friends of liberty, lies under an *odium* at present; but their arguments would be much clearer, and lose nothing of their strength; and their ideas would be more free from confusion, if they would openly maintain, that a certain *degree* of persecution was just, though certain degrees of it were unjust; and they might easily say, that they could not pretend to fix any precise boundary in this case, but must leave it to be determined by circumstances.

SECTION VII.

Farther observations concerning the extent of ecclesiastical authority, and the power of civil governors in matters of religion.

IT is said that a *christian church*, or a christian society, and the *power* of christian societies, are certainly spoken of in the New Testament; that societies cannot subsist without *officers* and *laws*, nor can laws be enforced without *penalties*. All this, and every consequence of the like nature, is readily granted; but the sanctions of the church of Christ in this world are, like itself, and like the *weapons of the christian warfare, not carnal*, and temporal, but of a *spiritual* nature; and do not affect a man's person, life, liberty, or estate. All that our Saviour directs, in case of the greatest refractoriness, is to consider such obstinate offenders as *heathen men and publicans*; that is, we are justified in ceasing to look upon them as brethren and fellow christians; and they are not intitled to our peculiar affection, and attention, as such.

The *delivering over to Satan*, which St Paul mentions,[25] as a punishment for the greatest offence that could be committed in the christian church, is not a delivering over to the *civil magistrate*, or to the *executioner*. In short, all that the New Testament authorizes a christian church, or its officers, to do, is to exclude from their society those persons whom they deem unworthy of it. There is no hint of such excluded members lying under any civil disqualification. If they were not to be considered as *christians*, and proper members of christian societies; they were still *men*, proper members of civil society, and not liable to civil penalties, unless they had, likewise, offended against the laws of the state.

The horrid sentence of *excommunication*, as it is in use in the church of Rome, or the church of England, is well known not to have been introduced into the christian church, till the Roman Emperors became christians; and was not established in its full extent till about the fifth century, when it was adopted by the barbarous Celtes, and other Germanic nations, and made similar to what they had practised in their own Druidical religion; which was, in this respect, analogous to that of the Hindoos. In both of them excommunication was the heaviest punishment that could be incurred in human society, as it cut a man off from all the benefits of it.

It will be said that, in the times of St Paul, temporal penalties were inflicted upon members of the christian church, for their irregularities committed in it. *For this cause*, says the apostle, *some are weak and sickly among you, and some sleep*[26] which is generally understood to refer to sickness and death, as a punishment for their shameful abuse of the institution of the Lord's supper. But it should be considered, that

[25] I Corinthians 5: 5.   [26] I Corinthians 11: 30.

these punishments were the immediate *act of God*, and in the strictest sense miraculous, like the death of Ananias and Sapphira, or the blindness of Elymas the sorcerer. These cases, therefore, will not authorize punishments inflicted by men. All that can be done to those who are guilty of contempt against church power, is to leave them to the *judgment of God*, who will sufficiently protect his church, and who is a better judge of its real danger than man can be; and if he choose to bear with such offenders, what have we to do to obstruct the effects of his long suffering and mercy?

I have no objection, however, on my own account, to allowing ecclesiastical officers to do more than Christ, than St Paul, or the other apostles ever pretended to. Let them not only *predict*, but, if their zeal prompt them to it, let them *imprecate* divine judgments. Let them pray that *God would speedily plead his own cause*, taking it for granted to be their own. Were I the obnoxious person, I should be very easy upon the occasion, provided their own cruel and merciless hands were not upon me.

It is allowed by many, that christian churches, as such, and its officers, as such, have no right to inflict civil punishments; but they say the civil magistrate may embrace the christian religion, and enforce its precepts by civil penalties. But have civil magistrates, when they become christians, a power of altering, or new modelling the christian religion, any more than other members of the christian church? If not, its laws and sanctions remain just as they did before, such as Jesus Christ and his apostles left them; and the things that may have been substituted in their place, cannot be called christianity, but are something else.

If the civil magistrate choose to become a christian, by all means let the doors of the christian church be open to him, as they ought to be to all, without distinction or respect of persons; but when he is in, let him be considered as no more than any other private christian. Give him a vote in all cases in which the whole assembly is concerned, but let him, like others, be subject to church censures, and even to be excommunicated, or excluded for notorious ill behaviour.

It is, certainly, contrary to all ideas of common sense, to suppose that civil magistrates embracing christianity have, therefore, a power of making laws for the christian church, and enforcing the observance of them by sanctions altogether unsuitable to its nature. The idea cannot be admitted without supposing a total change in the very first principles and essentials of christianity. If civil penalties be introduced into the christian church, it is, in every sense, and to every purpose, making it a *kingdom of this world*. Its governors then assume a power over men's persons and property, a power unknown in the institutes of our religion. If, moreover, the civil magistrate take upon him to prescribe creeds and confessions of faith, as is the case in England, what is it but to usurp a *dominion over the faith of christians*, a power, which the apostles themselves expressly disclaimed.

It may be said, that the civil magistrate, upon embracing christianity, and being convinced of the excellency of its precepts, may choose to incorporate them into his scheme of civil policy, and enforce them by civil penalties, not as matters of religion, but as belonging to civil government. Thus Christ has forbidden polygamy, and the civil magistrate (a Turk for instance) being converted to christianity, in order to put an end to the former custom, may make it death to marry two wives. He may also think the ministers of the christian church a very respectable order of men, and invest them with civil power; whereby they may be enabled to inflict civil punishments, in cases where, before, they could only make use of admonitions; and he may tax the people for their support. Thinking one mode of christianity preferable to another, may he not also, arm its ministers, with a civil power for suppressing the rest; when, before, they could only have used arguments for this purpose? Are civil and ecclesiastical powers so very incompatible that the same persons may not be invested with both? Were not all heads of families, both *kings* and *priests*, in the patriarchal times?

I answer, that, whatever regulations the civil magistrate may adopt, yet, as his adopting of them, and enforcing them by civil penalties makes them, confessedly, to be of a civil nature, he is not intitled to obedience with respect to them, so far as they are of a religious nature. If, therefore, any private christian should differ in opinion from his civil magistrate, or those invested by him with civil power, with respect to those things which are of a religious nature, he cannot consider himself as under any more obligation to submit to him, than he would be to submit to a heathen magistrate in the same case. A conscientious christian will never hesitate about obeying God rather than man, though that man should be a magistrate, or though he should be a christian, and assume the title of supreme head of the whole, or any part of the christian church. Any other maxims than these, it is evident, might be attended with the utter subversion of the christian religion. For the civil magistrate would have nothing to do but to adopt christianity into his system of civil policy; and then, having the whole within his own cognizance, he might add and alter at pleasure, till he had made it quite a different thing from what he found it.

It is upon this principle of the civil magistrate converting christianity into civil policy, or something similar to it, that Dr Balguy, and, I believe, most of the advocates for church power in England at present, found their claim to ecclesiastical authority. The clergy of former ages went upon quite another ground. They claimed authority *jure divino*, and scorned to derive their power from the civil magistrate. These two species of authority were perpetually opposed to one another; and the church encroached upon the state, or the state upon the church, as opportunity favoured their respective attempts; insomuch that the history of Europe, in the dark ages, is little more than an account of the violent struggles between these two contrary powers.

The Romish clergy still keep up the same pretences, and so did the clergy of the church of England, till they were fairly argued, or laughed out of them. Upon this, they have, lately, set up another claim to power, not *contrary to*, but *under* that of the civil magistrate. In their present ideas, the ecclesiastical establishment is a *creature of the state*. They consider themselves as *civil officers*, employed by the king to teach the religion the state has adopted, and they receive their wages, as other servants of the crown.

Now, admitting all this, what have the people to do with them as ministers of the gospel, and servants of Jesus Christ; since *they teach for doctrines the commandments of men?*[27] Hitherto the christian people of this country have imagined, that their ministers came to them with a commission from Christ, to teach them the things that relate to their everlasting happiness, and thereby secure the salvation of their immortal souls. Hitherto they have held them in reverence as successors of the apostles, and *submitted themselves* to them, as to persons, *who watched for their souls, as those who must give an account to their chief shepherd, when he shall appear,*[28] and who, for their good, were invested with spiritual power, independent of all human authority.

---

[27]Matthew 15: 9; Mark 7: 7.   [28]Hebrews 13: 17.

Should they not now, therefore, be apprized, that their ghostly superiors have, of late, renounced the principle on which they have hitherto yielded them obedience, and that their clergy choose to rank with justices of the peace, and other civil and crown officers, that they may, accordingly, change the mode of respect they have hitherto paid them?

Not that I wonder that the advocates for the church of England have changed the ground of their defence, and that they are not a little embarrassed with their *temporal supreme head*. It was a thing that was quite *new* in the christian church, a thing that was by no means their own choice, originally, but was forced upon them, and what they are now obliged to make the best of; so that if one hypothesis will not support the innovation, they must have recourse to another.

At this day, articles of faith, and rules of church discipline are enacted, and liable to be abrogated by acts of parliament; whereas all this business was formerly done in synods, and general councils, which acknowledged less dependence on the civil power; and, low as is my opinion of the persons who composed the synods, and general councils of former times, I cannot help thinking them more competent judges of articles of christian faith than any *king of England*, assisted, or not assisted by an *English parliament*. When these temporal powers shall think proper to *enact* any more ecclesiastical canons, or confessions of faith, I hope that, for the sake of decency, they will purge the two houses of those members who cannot give satisfactory evidence that they are christians at all. But, upon recollection, Dr Balguy will not think this circumstance necessary, since, according to his determination, the civil magistrate is not to provide for himself, but for the *largest sect* among his subjects; and therefore a Mahometan magistrate might be as safely trusted to make christian constitutions as any christian magistrate whatever. Perhaps he might be thought more proper, since, having no bias in favour of any particular sect of christians, he might be expected to be a more impartial judge in the case.

The reason which the Bishop of Gloucester gives for the propriety of making the civil magistrate the supreme head of the church, "whereby he becomes possessed of the sole right of ordering and decreeing every thing that the ministers and officers of the church had before a power of doing, (so that even all matters of opinion are out of

74

the jurisdiction of the church)" is really curious. "The church," it seems, "wants protection from external violence. This protection the state only can give to it; but," says this author, "protection not being to be afforded to any person or body, without power over that person or body, in the person or body protecting, it necessarily follows, that the civil magistrate must be supreme."

I cannot help thinking that the church, according to this author, made a very hard bargain, and paid very dear for protection. Might not the state have been content to *protect* the church, without *dictating* to her in ecclesiastical matters? Certainly at the time this famous alliance was made, the agents for the church were under a panic, and must have forgotten that Christ himself had promised to protect his church, to be with it to the end of the world, and that the gates of hell should not prevail against it.

Were it not for the power to favour the professors of religion with which magistrates are invested, one might wonder how, of all mankind, they should ever have been thought of, as proper to take the lead in an affair of this nature. I should much sooner have thought of applying to them to superintend the business of medicine, in which the healths and lives of their subjects are so much concerned. But, happily for mankind, they have not taken it into their heads to inter-meddle so much with it. The reason is, that there is nothing in the business of medicine, of which they could avail themselves; whereas a league with *priests*, who have always a great influence over mankind, has often been extremely convenient for them.

Of all mankind, surely magistrates have the least leisure, and the least capacity for judging in matters of religion. Consequently, they are most likely to determine rashly, and in such a manner as best suits with their worldly views. Of this we have a notable example in the Hampton-Court conference. There the advocates for presbyterian-ism and episcopacy had a solemn meeting, to debate on the merits of their respective modes of church government, in the presence of King James I. (of blessed memory in the church of England) at a time, when, perhaps, a majority of the nation were disposed in favour of presbyterianism. But was a king, with his head full of the notions of arbitrary power, in a proper disposition to decide a controversy of this nature: and might it not have been expected, that the maxim *No bishop no king* would be sufficient to determine his choice, against the weight of a thousand solid arguments. The issue of the conference is well known, but no better than it was before it took place. Such cause have the advocates for episcopacy to boast of their triumph!

The history of this Hampton-Court controversy,[29] so admirably exemplifies the reasoning of the Bishop of Gloucester, that I wonder it was not adduced by him, in aid of his argument to prove, that the civil magistrate is more likely to decide according to truth in matters of religion than churchmen. Let us hear the great champion himself on this subject, as this part of his argument seems to be the great hinge on which the most important part of the controversy concerning establishments, turns. "Church sanctity being acquired by secession, and retirement from human affairs, and that secession rendering men ignorant of civil society, its rights and interests (in the place of which will succeed all the follies of superstition and fanaticism) we must needs conclude that religion, under such directors and reformers, will deviate from truth, and consequently a capacity, in proportion, of serving society. On the other hand, when religion comes under the magistrate's directions, its purity must needs be well supported and preserved. For truth and public utility coinciding, the civil magistrate, as such, will see it for his interest to seek after and promote truth in religion, and by means of public utility, which his office enables him so well to understand, he will never be at a loss to know where such truth is to be found, so that it is impossible, under this civil influence, for religion ever to deviate far from truth." *Risum teneatis amici!*[30]

I shall only observe, in answer to this curious piece of reasoning, that in an *advertisement* prefixed to this very work, he says, "It is a trite observation, that divines make bad politicians. I believe it is more generally true, that politicians are but bad divines." A confession which, I own, I should not have expected from a man who, in the very same book, pleads for the propriety of making these same *politicians*, alias *bad divines*, the final judges in all ecclesiastical causes, and for giving them a power of enacting articles of faith and ecclesiastical canons.

This author, indeed, thinks there is a necessity for churchmen making part the legislative body, lest, instead of being *subjects*, they should be the *slaves* of the state, p. 78. But so long as the bishops in

---

[29] The Hampton Court Conference of 1604 placed James I in the role of arbiter between spokesmen for the puritan and more mainstream wings of the Established Church.
[30] 'You may smile, my friends.'

parliament have no negative upon the resolutions of the house (a privilege which this bishop himself would not allow them) I do not see what their feat there would avail them, if all the laity should differ from them in their opinion concerning religious matters. In this case, ecclesiastical canons would be made, and articles of faith enacted, as contrary to their inclinations, as if they had not been consulted at all. So that, in case of an opposition between the two powers, the clergy are still entirely at the mercy of the laity, and therefore their slaves.

Upon the whole, considering every thing relating to this new business of a temporal head over christians, who are expressly commanded to *call no man master upon earth*[31] and considering how averse the clergy always were to such a catastrophe in their affairs, and how little they were prepared for it; I cannot help thinking, that they have given very striking proofs of their acuteness, and presence of mind, in defending it so plausibly as they have done.

To make this case of a temporal head to a spiritual church the more intelligible, let us suppose there are, in any country, a number of persons, who have formed themselves into a society for promoting natural philosophy; that the civil magistrate hears of it, and, having a taste for the study, becomes a member. If, upon this, he should take upon him to make laws for the society, and to enforce them with civil penalties; or if he should compel the members to subscribe to particular propositions, and hypotheses, should we not pronounce that the philosophical society was, to all intents and purposes, dissolved? In like manner a christian magistrate, pretending to make laws to the christian church, is to be considered as doing every thing in his power to abolish christianity, and setting up something else in its place, that may be more or less like it, just as it shall happen.

It may be said that an union of civil and ecclesiastical power may take place in another manner, namely by a nation of christians voluntarily choosing the civil magistrate to be their protector or head, and to make laws for them. So also a society of philosophers may choose the civil magistrate for their protector and head; but if, in this case, he should compel their assent to his own opinions, would it not be thought that, notwithstanding their choice of the civil magistrate for their head, if they submitted to his impositions, they ceased to be what they were before, and the society changed its nature and character! In

---

[31] Matthew 23: 9.

like manner, christians act altogether out of character in choosing a temporal head; and no person who has a just regard to his religion, and *the liberty wherewith Christ has made him free*,[32] will ever acknowledge such a dependence on the civil power.

Whenever, therefore, the civil magistrate, either in consequence of becoming a member of the christian church, by incorporating christianity into his system of civil policy, or by being chosen supreme head of the church in a christian nation, introduces into the gospel such laws and sanctions as are evidently unsuitable to the nature of it; as, for instance, when, instead of voluntary contributions to the church stock, he appoints the compulsory payment of dues; and when, for exhortation and reproof, he substitutes fines and confiscations, torture and death, this new modelled scheme cannot be called christianity. Thus when the poor in England became intitled to a legal maintenance, charity, on which they before subsisted, was so far precluded; for a man who now pays a poor rate is not to be ranked with him who *gives alms of that which he possesses*.[33] In all cases a change in the fundamental maxims of government, especially a change both in the laws themselves, and in the sanctions of them, cannot be deemed less than a change in the constitution.

For my own part, I can conceive no method whatever, in which the civil magistrate can be invested with ecclesiastical power, or ecclesiastics with civil power, so that a conscientious christian shall consider himself as under any obligation to yield them obedience in their new character. In civil matters he will obey the civil magistrate, and where religion is concerned, he will listen to nothing but the dictates of his own conscience, or the admonitions of his chosen spiritual guide; and to him no farther than he is satisfied he has a better authority than his own for what he says. However they agree to change or mix their powers, their alliance and stipulations will have no weight with him. He will still *give to Cæsar the things that are Cæsar's and unto God the things that are God's*[34] and he will judge for himself, what are the things that are due to the one or the other. If he should make any mistake in this case, it will be some apology for him, that his superiors had confounded his understanding, by the unnatural mixture they had made of things of such different natures.

Had there been such a connection between ecclesiastical and civil

[32]Galatians 5:1. [33]Luke 12: 33.
[34]Matthew 22: 21; Mark 12: 17; Luke 20: 25.

matters, as the advocates for church power contend for; had it been the proper office of the civil magistrate to superintend the affairs of religion, and had it been unlawful, as some assert, for private persons to attempt any alteration in it, except by application to the civil governor; is it not unaccountable, that our Lord, and his apostles, did not make their first proposals to the supreme magistrates among the Jews or Romans? They certainly had no idea of the peculiar obligation of magistrates to attend to this business, and to choose a religion for the people, since we never hear of their making application to them on any such account. It was their constant custom to preach the gospel wherever they came, in all companies, and to all persons promiscuously; and almost all the intercourse they had with magistrates, seems to have been on occasion of their being brought before them as criminals.

Our Lord sent out, both his twelve apostles, and also seventy disciples, among all the cities of Israel, but we do not read of his sending any deputation to the rulers of the Jews. John the Baptist seems to have confined his preaching to the wilderness of Judea, and the territory in the neighbourhood of the river Jordan; where he gave his exhortations to all that came to hear him, without distinction of persons. St Paul, indeed, made an appeal to Cæsar, but it was in order to obtain his liberty in an unjust prosecution. We are not informed that he, or any of the apostles, ever took any measures to lay the evidences of the christian religion before the Roman emperor, or the Roman senate, in order to convince them of the truth and excellency of it, and induce them to abolish heathenism, in favour of it, throughout the Roman empire; which many persons would now think to have been the readiest, the most proper, and the best method of christianizing the world. On the contrary, their whole conduct shows, that they considered religion as the proper and immediate concern of every single person, and that there was no occasion whatever to consult, or advise with any earthly superior in a case of this nature.

If magistrates had a right to choose a mode of religion for their people, much more, one would think, had *masters* a right to choose for their *slaves* in this case; yet we find great numbers of converts were made amongst this most dependent part of mankind, without any account of their masters being consulted, or applied to about it. The contrary is clearly inferred, from the first view of things, in primitive times.

Though it be true, that we must not expect to find in the scriptures an accurate account of every thing belonging to a christian church, including a minute description of the rank and power of its officers, it does not therefore follow, that it is not worth our while to consult them on this subject; for we shall find such a general view of the mutual relations, and reciprocal duties of christians, as may prevent our making any considerable mistake, with respect to the authority of some, or the subjection of others.

It cannot be inferred from any thing that our Saviour has delivered, that any one christian has a right authoritatively to dictate or prescribe to another, but I think the very contrary, if it be in the power of words to convey such a meaning.

If we consider the plan of the primitive church, we shall see that it was evidently formed upon that of the Jewish synagogue; in which the *elders* (all of whom promiscuously instructed the rest) were persons of the greatest age and experience, and he that is called the *ruler of the synagogue* (to which the office of the christian *bishop* corresponds) was only one of them, distinguished, indeed, by some titles of honour, but with no superior power worth mentioning. This is the reason why both the rulers of the synagogues among the Jews, and bishops in christian churches, are generally called elders, in common with the rest. The office of deacon was also the same in both, and needs no description in this place.

The apostles always represent themselves as appointed witnesses of the life, sufferings, and resurrection of Christ; but, seem not to have arrogated any dominion over the faith of their fellow christians.

So far were they from assuming any authority over their brethren, or peremptorily enjoining any thing of themselves, except they were authorized to do it by the immediate direction of the Holy Ghost, that they virtually disclaimed all such power; and when their advice was not taken, and their designs obstructed, they wrote as persons who had nothing but reason on their side, without dictating, or giving themselves such airs as modern dignitaries in the church would assume, in case of such opposition.

SECTION VIII.

Of the necessity, or utility, of ecclesiastical establishments.

[[35]The friends and advocates for church power, generally found their system on the necessity of establishing some religion or other, agreeably, they say, to the custom of all wise nations. This being admitted, it is evident, they think, that the supreme civil magistrate must have the choice of this religion, and being thus lodged in the hands of the chief magistrate, it is easily and effectually guarded. Thus the propriety of a most rigid *intolerance*, and the most abject *passive obedience* are presently, and clearly inferred; so that the people have no right to relieve themselves from ecclesiastical oppressions, except by petition to their temporal and spiritual governors, whose interest it generally is to continue every abuse that the people can complain of.

But before this admirably connected system can be admitted, a few things should be previously considered. And I am aware that, if they had been duly attended to, the system either would never have taken place, or it would have been so moderated, when put into execution, as that it would never have been worth the while of its advocates to contend so zealously for it.

1. All the rational plea for ecclesiastical establishments, is founded on the necessity of them, in order to enforce obedience to civil laws; but though religious considerations be allowed to be an excellent *aid* to civil sanctions, it will not, therefore, follow, as some would gladly have it understood, that, therefore, the business of civil government could not have been carried on *at all* without them. I do not know how it is, that this position seems, in general, to have passed without dispute or examination; but, for my own part, I see no reason to think that civil society could not have subsisted, and even have subsisted

---

[35]New material continues to p. 87.

very well, without the aid of any foreign sanctions. I am even satisfied that, in many countries, the junction of civil and ecclesiastical powers hath done much mischief, and that it would have been a great blessing to the bulk of the people, if their magistrates had never interfered in matters of religion at all, but had left them to provide for themselves in that respect, as they generally do, with regard to medicine.

"There are," says the bishop of Gloucester, "a numerous set of duties of *imperfect obligation*, which human laws could not reach. This can only be done by an ecclesiastical jurisdiction, intrusted by the state with coercive power. And indeed the supplying that defect, which these courts do supply, was the original and fundamental motive of the state seeking this alliance." But I would ask, Are not ecclesiastical officers *men*, mere human beings, possessed of only a limited power of discernment, as well as civil officers? Will they not, therefore, find themselves under the same difficulty in enforcing the duties of imperfect obligation, that the civil officers would have done, notwithstanding the coercive power they receive from the state for that purpose? In short, I do not see what an ecclesiastical court can do in this case, more than a civil court of equity. Is not this, in fact, confessed by this author, when he allows, p. 87, that "there must be an appeal from these courts to the civil, in all cases." For, if the civil courts be qualified to judge of these things, by appeal, why could they not have done it in the first instance?

2. If the expediency of ecclesiastical establishments be allowed, it is allowed on account of their *utility* only; and therefore, as there are infinite differences in the coercive power of these establishments, this reason will not justify their being carried to a greater extent than the good of society requires. And though it may be productive of, or, at least, consistent with the good of society, that the civil magistrate should give some degree of countenance to the professors of one sect of religion (which, with me, however, is extremely problematical) it were a gross perversion of all reasoning and common sense, to infer from thence, that the people should not have free liberty to dissent from this religion of their civil governor, or even to use any honest and fair method of gaining converts to what they should think to be the truth. Because whatever utility there may be in *ecclesiastical establishments*, there is certainly utility in *truth*, especially moral and religious truth; and truth can never have a fair chance of being discovered, or propagated, without the most perfect freedom of inquiry and debate.

Though it may be true, that there never was any country without some national religion, it is not true that these religions were always adopted with a view to aid the civil government. It appears to me that, with respect to the states of Greece, and other barbarous nations (for the Greeks were no better than their neighbours in this respect) motives of a very different nature from these; motives derived from nothing but the most blind and abject superstition, and the most groundless apprehensions, were those that really induced them to make such rigid provision for the perpetuity of their several religions. Their laws have not, in fact, any such intermixture of civil and religious matters, as is now found in the systems of European states. We do not find in them, that duties properly religious are enforced by civil sanctions, nor duties properly civil enforced by religious ones, in the senses in which we now use those terms, as if these things had, naturally, so necessary a connection. But in these ignorant and superstitious ages, men fancied there was what we should call an *arbitrary connection* between the observance of certain religious rites, and the continuance of certain states; and that the gods, who were particularly attentive to their preservation, would withdraw their protection, upon the disuse of those ceremonies.

The Bishop of Gloucester seems to agree with me in this, for he says, "The unity of the object of faith, and conformity to a formulary of dogmatic theology, as the terms of communion, is the great foundation and bond of religious society. Now this the several societies of pagan religion wanted, in which there was only a conformity in national ceremonies."

Had the ancient heathens entertained any such notion of the *direct* subserviency of religion to civil policy (*i.e.* in a *moral view*) as the advocates for church power endeavour to avail themselves of at this day, they would have made a distinction among religions. Whereas, it is plain they had no idea of the excellence of one mode of religion above another, as more conducive to the happiness of mankind (unless there was something peculiarly shocking in some of their rites, as that of sacrificing human victims) but they imagined that different rites, rites differing not in moral excellence, but in mere form, were necessary for different states; and that it was wrong, and hazardous, for two nations to interchange their religions.

Indeed, after these establishments had taken place, it is probable that some of the defenders of them, in ransacking their imaginations for arguments, might hit upon some such reasons as modern high churchmen have urged; but it no more follows from thence, that the establishments were originally founded on those principles, than that because plausible reasons may (for any thing I know) be alleged for the use of a *white surplice* in reading the prayers of the church, and for bishops wearing *mitres* and *lawn sleeves*,[36] that, therefore, Jesus Christ and his apostles used them.

4. [*sic*] Though there may be no christian country in which some species of christianity is not, more or less, established, *i.e.* more or less favoured by the government; yet there are countries in which less favour is shown to the prevailing mode than in others, and in which much less care is taken to guard it, as in Holland, Russia, Pensilvania, and I believe others of our American colonies. Now, let an enquiry be made into the state of these countries, and see whether the result of it will be favourable, or unfavourable to establishments. What *tendency to inconvenience* has there been observed in those states in which church government is most relaxed, and what *superior advantages*, in point of real happiness, are enjoyed in those countries in which it is strained to the highest pitch. I have no doubt of the result of such an inquiry turning out greatly in favour of the relaxation of religious establishments, if not of their total suppression. A just view of all the real evils that attend the ecclesiastical establishment in England, with respect to *knowledge, virtue, commerce*, and many other things with which the happiness of states is connected, but more especially with respect to *liberty*, would be sufficient to deter any legislator from introducing any thing like it into a new state; unless, without thinking at all, he took it for granted that there was no doing without one, or was so weak as to be frighted by the mere clamour of bigots.

5. Though it may be true, that inconvenience would arise from the immediate suppression of religious establishments, it doth not therefore follow, that they were either necessary or expedient; that the nation would have been in a worse state if they had never existed; and that no measures ought to be taken to relax or dissolve them. Were the religion of Mahomet abolished every where at once, no doubt much confusion would be occasioned; yet what christian would, for that reason, wish for the perpetuity of that superstition? The same may be said of popery, and many other kinds of corrupt religion.

---

[36] 'Lawn sleeves' was a derisory description of the balloon sleeves on a bishop's gown.

Customs, of whatever kind, that have prevailed so long as to have influenced the genius and manners of a whole nation, cannot be changed without trouble. Such a shock to men's prejudices would necessarily give them pain, and unhinge them for a time. It is the same with vicious habits of the body, which terminate in diseases and death; but must they be indulged, and the fatal consequences calmly expected, because the patient would find it painful and difficult to alter his method of living? Ecclesiastical establishments, therefore, may be a real *evil*, and a disease in civil society, and a dangerous one too, notwithstanding all the arguments for the support of them, derived from the confusion and inconvenience attending their dissolution; so far is this consideration from proving them to be things excellent or useful in themselves.

Even the mischiefs that might be apprehended from attempts to amend or dissolve establishments, are much aggravated by writers. Much less opposition, I am persuaded, would arise from the source of real *bigotry*, than from the quarter of *interest*, and the bigotry that was set in motion by persons who were not themselves bigots.

It is imagined by some, that christianity could not have subsisted without the aid of the civil powers, and that the dissolution of its establishment would endanger its very being. The Bishop of Gloucester, says, that "the state was induced to seek an alliance with the church, as the necessary means of preserving the being of religion;" and that "all the advantage the church expects from the alliance with the state, can be no other than security from all outward violence;" "it being impertinent," as he justly observes, "in the church to aim at riches, honours, and power; because these are things which, as a church, she can neither use, nor receive profit from." He also says, "that religion could not operate for want of a common arbiter, who had impartiality to apply the rule of right, and power to enforce its operations." But these persons seem not to be acquainted with its proper *internal strength*, or they would not lay so much stress on such poor and heterogeneous supports. They should consider how the christian religion was supported, without the help of any establishment, before the time of Constantine. Is it not true, in fact, that it not only subsisted, but amazingly increased in all that period; when it was so far from being protected by civil authority, that all human powers were combined against it?

If they say it was supported by miracles in all that interval, it behoves them to make good the assertion. On the contrary, it appears from church history, that when christianity was once established, (if I may use that term) by the preaching and miracles of the apostles, it was able afterwards to support itself by its own evidence. And this evidence is still sufficient to support it, though all the powers on earth, and the gates of hell, were combined against it. Certainly those who make use of this plea for christian establishments seem to insinuate, that christianity is destitute of *sufficient evidence*; and could not advance any thing more favourable to the purpose of its most inveterate enemies.

One circumstance in favour of my argument is very evident. If the support of christianity had not been piously undertaken by Constantine, and the succeeding Roman emperors, the Popish hierarchy, that great *mystery of iniquity*, and *abomination*, could never have existed. And I think, all the advocates for church power, will not be able to mention any evil attending the want of ecclesiastical establishments, equal to this, which flowed from one.

All other ecclesiastical establishments among christians, partake more or less of the nature of this, the first and greatest of them, being nothing more than corrections and emendations of it. Many of the abuses in it have been rectified, but many of them, also, are retained in them all. That there are some things good and useful in them all is true, but it is no difficult matter to point out many things that are good (that is, which have been attended with consequences beneficial to mankind) in the grossest abuses of popery. Those who study history cannot fail to be acquainted with them, and there is no occasion to point them out in this place.

Thanks to the excellent constitution of things, that there is no acknowledged evil in the whole course of nature, or providence, that is without a beneficial operation, sufficient to justify the appointment or permission of it, by that great and good Being who made, and who superintends all things. But because tempests by land and sea, poisonous plants and animals, &c. do good, considered as parts of the whole system; and because it certainly seems better in the sight of God, that they should exist than not, must we not, therefore, guard against their pernicious effects to ourselves?

Let this be applied to the case of civil and ecclesiastical tyranny in every form. The Divine Being, for wise and good ends, permits them; but he has given us a power to oppose them, and to guard ourselves against them. And we need not doubt, but that things will be so guided by his unseen hand, that the good they were intended to answer will be answered, notwithstanding our just opposition; or will appear to *have been* answered, if we succeed in putting a final end to them. He makes use of men, as his instruments, both in establishing, and removing all these abuses in civil and ecclesiastical government.]

Ecclesiastical authority may have been necessary in the infant state of society; and, for the same reason, it may, perhaps, continue to be, in some degree, necessary as long as society is imperfect; and therefore may not be entirely abolished, till civil government have arrived at a much greater degree of perfection.

If, therefore, I were asked, whether I should approve of the immediate dissolution of all the ecclesiastical establishments in Europe, I should answer, no. This might, possibly, especially in some countries, for reasons that cannot be foreseen, be too hazardous an experiment. To begin with due caution, let experiments be first made of *alterations*; or, which is the same thing, of *better establishments* than the present. Let them be reformed in many essential articles, and then not thrown aside entirely, till it be found by experience, that no good can be made of them. If I be asked in what particulars I imagine them to be most deficient, and what *kind* of reformation I could wish to have made in them; I answer, I could wish they were reformed in the four following respects, which are all of a capital nature, and in which almost all our present establishments are fundamentally wrong; as I make no doubt will appear to every man, of common sense, who shall give the least attention to this subject.

1. Let the articles of faith, to be subscribed by candidates for the ministry, be greatly reduced. In the formulary of the church of England, might not thirty-eight out of the thirty-nine be very well spared? It is a reproach to any christian establishment, if every man cannot claim the benefit of it, who can say, that he believes in the religion of *Jesus Christ*, as it is set forth in the *New Testament*. You say the terms are so general, that even deists would quibble, and insinuate themselves. I answer, that all the articles which are subscribed at present, by no means exclude deists who will prevaricate; and upon this scheme you would at least exclude fewer honest men. But all temptation to prevaricate will be taken away if the next article of reformation be attended to.

2. Let the livings of the clergy be made more equal, in proportion to

the duty required of each: and when the stipend is settled, let not the importance of the office be estimated above its real value. Let nothing be considered but the work, and the necessary expenses of a liberal education.

3. Let the clergy be confined to their ecclesiastical duty, and have nothing to do in conducting affairs of state. Is not their presence in the cabinet rather dangerous? The seat of our bishops in parliament is a relic of the popish usurpations over the temporal rights of the sovereigns of Europe; and is not every thing of this nature justly considered as a great absurdity in modern government? The question, by what right they sit, need not be discussed. As teachers of the religion of Christ, whose kingdom was not of this world, can they have any business to meddle with civil government? However, if they be allowed to sit in the great council of the nation, as members of the community at large; suppose they were fairly elected like other members; but let not such a civil power as they now have devolve upon them, as a matter of course, on any pretence whatever.

4. Let the system of *toleration* be completely carried into execution: and let every member of the community enjoy every right of a citizen, whether he choose to conform to the established religion or not. Let every man, who has sufficient abilities, be deemed qualified to serve his country in any civil capacity. Because a man cannot be a *bishop*, must he therefore be *nothing* in the state, and his country derive no benefit from his talents? Besides, let it be considered, that those who depart the farthest from established opinions will have more at stake in a country where they enjoy these singular privileges; and, consequently, will be more attached to it.

The toleration in England, notwithstanding our boasted liberty, is far from being complete. Our present laws do not tolerate those more rational dissenters, whom the bishop of Gloucester looks upon as brethren. It is known to every body, that if the toleration act was strictly put in execution, it would silence all those dissenting ministers who are held in any degree of esteem by the church; in the same manner as a truly conscientious subscription to the thirty-nine articles would silence almost all that are rational, and free from enthusiasm, among themselves. it is not the law, but the mildness of the administration, and the spirit of the times, to which we are indebted for our present liberties. But the man who should attempt to abuse the letter of the law, contrary to the spirit of the times, and in order to trample upon the sacred rights of humanity, will ever be infamous.

The most unexceptionable establishment of religion that I have yet heard of is that of some of our North-American colonies, in which all the inhabitants are obliged to pay a tax for the support of some form of the christian religion, but every man's contribution is faithfully applied to the use of whatever church, or society, he himself shall choose. To such an ecclesiastical establishment as this, few persons, I believe, in the present state of things would have much objection. It would not indeed be perfect and unbounded liberty in matters of religion; but it would be pretty near it, and might make way for it.

[I do not mean, therefore, to plead against religious establishments in all cases; but only argue against fixing every thing so unalterably, that if a change, in any particular, should be desired by a great majority of the clergy, or laity themselves, they should not be able to accomplish it, without the danger of throwing every thing into confusion. Such rigid establishments imply the authors of them to have been well persuaded of their own infallibility; or rather that they were determined to enforce every measure once adopted, notwithstanding the fullest conviction of its being a bad one. For no man, who could suppose it possible for himself to be mistaken, would think of setting up his opinions as the invariable standard for posterity; and none but the founder of a Median or Persian establishment would think it was reasonable, that, after a mistake was discovered in his system, and universally acknowledged to be such, all persons (if they would enjoy any advantage under it) should be obliged to affirm, that they believed it to be no mistake, but perfectly agreeable to truth.

How far this is the case with the church of England, let those of her clergy say, who may understand the subject of religion a little better than the first reformers, just emerging from the darkness of popery; who may have some reluctance to subscribe what they do not believe, and who may feel, notwithstanding every evasion to which they can have recourse, that a church preferment is dearly bought at the expense of a solemn falsehood. I do not appeal to those who may really believe all they subscribe, or to those who may subscribe without thinking at all, or to those who would wait upon any minister of state in the world with a *carte blanche* ready signed. In saying this, I even hint no more than what many of the greatest ornaments of the church have said again and again; that some things, in our present establishment, are wrong, and want reformation; and that there are thinking and unthinking, honest and dishonest men in this, as well as in every other profession.

I doubt not, the wisest and the most worthy of the English prelates would rather see the privileges of the dissenters enlarged than abridged, in any important article; for, allowing their dissent to be ever so unreasonable, there is no man who has the least knowledge of history or of human nature, but must be sensible, that the very distinguished reputation which the body of the English clergy enjoy at present is, not a little, owing to the existence and respectable figure of the protestant dissenters. Several of the most discerning of the English bishops have given their testimony, directly or indirectly, to this truth; particularly, if I remember right, bishop Gibson, in his charges to the clergy of his diocese. The present state of the dissenting interest can give no alarm to the established clergy with respect to their temporalities; and, certainly, the interests of religious knowledge, which all wise and good men of every denomination have most at heart, cannot fail to be promoted by that spirit of emulation, which will always subsist betwixt scholars and writers in two opposite persuasions.

There is no power on earth, but has grown exorbitant when it has met with no control. What was the character of the Romish clergy before the reformation? how shamefully ignorant, imperious, lazy, and debauched were the bulk of them! whereas very great numbers of them are now sensible, moderate, and virtuous; and little, in comparison, of the old leaven remains, except in Spain and Portugal, where the clergy have no intercourse with protestants, which might call forth an exertion of their faculties, and check the extravagance of their appetites and passions. To say that the English clergy, in future time, would not run into the vices, and sink into the contempt, into which the Romish clergy were sunk before the reformation, when they were in the same circumstances, would be to say they were not men.

It is Puffendorf, I think, who accounts for the great superiority of the English clergy over the Swedish upon this principle. In Sweden, though it be a protestant country, no dissenters are allowed; and their clergy have never produced any thing, in ethics or divinity, that deserves notice. Whoever made the observation, there is no doubt of the fact.

A few among the inferior clergy may wish the extinction of the dissenting interest, and might be ready to gratify their zeal, by persecuting those of their brethren whose consciences are, more tender than their own; but, certainly, there would not be wanting, in this age, men enough of more humanity, of juster sentiments, and of more enlarged views, among the higher ranks in the church, who would, with indignation, snatch the torch from their misguided hands. The indelible infamy which would, to the latest posterity, pursue the man, who should form, countenance, or even connive at, persecuting measures, in this age of moderation and good sense, will effectually deter men of understanding, and of a just knowledge of the world from these measures; and it is hoped, that men of zeal without knowledge will want abilities and influence to carry such schemes into execution.]

SECTION IX.

A review of some particular positions of Dr *Balguy*'s on the subject of church-authority

Several of the considerations mentioned in the preceding section were suggested by the perusal of Dr Balguy's sermon; and, I flatter myself, are sufficient to refute any arguments that he has produced in favour of *church-authority*. I shall, however, just descant upon a few passages in his performance, where we discover the great hinges on which his whole scheme turns.

"Not only," says he, p.8. "must persons be appointed for the performance of religious duties, but the manner also is to be prescribed. The assembly may not unfrequently be deceived in their choice, and the ministers, if subject to no restraint, may introduce principles and practices which the people condemn. Or it may happen that one minister shall pursue a different plan from another, perhaps a contrary plan; which must evidently tend to confound the minds of the people, and weaken the impressions of religion. If the difference be not in form only, but in doctrine, the case will still be worse; for nothing is so apt to root out all religion, both from men's heads and hearts, as religious controversy. Here then," says he, "we have the first sketch of what may be called, not improperly, *church-authority*."

As the inconveniences arising from the want of church-authority are here referred to, as the reason for ecclesiastical establishments, let us briefly examine whether they are not much exaggerated by this author; and, on the other hand, just point out a few of the inconveniences attending establishments, which he has not so much as hinted at, that the one may be fairly weighed against the other. In this I shall not content myself with mere *theory*, as Dr Balguy does, since there are known *facts* to refer to, as examples in both cases.

Among the Dissenters, if a minister introduce principles and practices which the people condemn, they dismiss him from their service, and choose another more agreeable to them. If his difference of sentiment occasion any debate, the subject of the debate is thereby more thoroughly understood; and the worst that can happen is, that some of them separate, and form themselves into a new society, or join another in their neighbourhood, that is more to their liking. In this, as in all other contests, some ill blood is produced, the effects of which may remain for some time; but the minds of the people in general are not so much confounded, nor the impressions of religion, as a principle of moral conduct, so much weakened as this writer imagines.

Among Dissenters, church emoluments are not worth contending for, and therefore those fierce contests *about* places, or *in* places, but seldom happen. A minister seldom chooses to be connected with a society whose general sentiments are much different from his own, nor do societies often invite a person to officiate among them without having previously sufficient reason to depend upon his being agreeable to them. Upon the whole, I am willing to appeal to any person who is well acquainted with the state of Dissenters in England, whether disagreeable events happen so often, or whether the worst effects are of so much consequence, as to bear being put in the balance with the capital advantages of their situation, for improving in religious knowledge and virtue.

Something of the spirit of controversy seems necessary to keep up men's attention to religion in general, as well as to other things; and, notwithstanding a fondness for debate may be of some disservice to practical religion, it is far less so than a total inattention to the subject. In theological and scriptural inquiries, the *practical* truths of christianity must necessarily present themselves to the mind. Besides there is hardly any branch of christian knowledge but is more or less of a practical nature, and suggests considerations that are of use to mend the heart and reform the life. Religious knowledge is, however, itself, as valuable an acquisition as knowledge of any other kind.

Some may think it an unhappiness that the common people should be so knowing in matters of religion. But this complaint is to be considered in the same light with the complaint of statesmen, in free countries, of the common people troubling themselves so much about *politics*; while the friend of his country and of mankind will not, upon the whole, be displeased with either of these circumstances; being sensible, that the one is some guard against the incroachments of civil, and the other of ecclesiastical tyranny.

As to the confusion that is occasioned in congregations, when they happen to be dissatisfied with their ministers, it is not to be compared, for its pernicious effects, to the almost perpetual squabbles, between the established clergy and their parishioners, about *tythes*. Few parishes in the country are without disputes upon this subject, which create a standing opposition of interest between the people and their spiritual guides.

Lastly, What inconvenience can be pointed out, as having actually taken place among Dissenters for want of a standing *confession of faith*, that can be named with the dreadful mischiefs that have arisen from enforcing subscription in the church of England. This precludes all free inquiry upon subjects of religion, and entails every error and abuse from generation to generation, so that a reformation can hardly take place without violence and blood.

If the emoluments of church livings be considerable, the temptation to prevaricate with conscience is, by this means, made too strong for the generality of those who have been educated for the church, and who are now incapable of getting their bread, at least, of making their fortune, in any other way. Also, what must the people think, to see those who are appointed to instruct them in the principles of religion and morality, solemnly subscribing to articles of faith which they are known to disbelieve and abhor; and who among the clergy, that read and think at all, are supposed to believe one-third

93

of the thirty-nine articles of the church of England? I have so good an opinion of Dr Balguy's good sense, notwithstanding the futility of his reasoning in this performance, as to think it is a thousand to one, but that he himself is an unbeliever in many of them.

One would have thought that the shocking abuses of the church of Rome might have served as a standing monument of the danger of church establishments; when that *mystery of iniquity* stands upon record, as having thereby got so firm a footing, as, for so many ages, to have set all the civil powers of Europe, and all the powers of reason too, at defiance.

Having seen what this author has been able to advance in favour of the necessity of ecclesiastical establishments, and church-authority, I shall follow him a little farther; and observe what he has to allege for bringing a number of christian societies into one common system, in order to lay a broader and firmer foundation for the power of the church. From this combination he expects, p. 11, 12, more *wisdom*, and *uniformity*, a greater *variety* of *candidates* for church officers, and *a better choice* of them. "These societies," he well observes, "must necessarily act by deputies, so that, at least, either single men, or small bodies of men, must be authorized to govern the church. There is no necessity," says he, "that the ministers of religion should be appointed by the people, and much expedience in a different method of appointment."

To me, all this appears mere imagination, and the supposed advantages of this elaborate scheme to be altogether contrary to fact. I should much sooner have imagined there might be much expedience in town officers not being chosen by their townsmen, than in the ministers of a christian church not being chosen by the congregation.

The nomination to church livings, except by the members of the church themselves, is a thing so absurd, that the idea of it never occurred for many centuries in the christian world; and we may venture to say, that it never could have entered into the head of any man, had not the revenues of the church grown so considerable, as to become worth the notice of the civil magistrate, who took advantage of them to oblige his creatures and dependants. The fruits of this method of proceeding are such as might have been expected from the manner of its introduction. The people belonging to the established church, are like the *vassals* of the Polish nobility, or the mere *live stock* of a farm, delivered over, as *parcel of the estate*, to every successive incumbent.

As to the wisdom of choice among candidates for the ministry, we see, in fact, that the interest of the people is not at all considered in it. The same interest is openly made for *church livings* as for places, or emoluments of any other kind; and being procured by the same means, they are enjoyed in the same manner, without any idea of obligation to the people from whom their revenue arises.

What reason there is, or would be, to boast of the happy effects of uniformity in a great *number of societies*, comprehending a whole kingdom, or the whole christian world, we may judge from the horrible evils, before recited, that attend the necessary methods of enforcing this uniformity in a single society; for these must be multiplied in proportion to the number. We see, in fact, much more good than harm is found to result from the diversities in dissenting congregations. They are extremely favourable to the advancement of religious knowledge, and they afford a fine opportunity for the exercise of christian candour and charity; the very possibility of which would be excluded in, what Dr Balguy would call, a complete and perfect establishment. Some inconveniences cannot fail to arise from the most favourable situation of things; but in this state of trial, the Divine Being has not provided for the prevention of vice by cutting off all occasions of virtue.

Besides, so wise is the constitution of human nature, that differences of opinion cannot be prevented by any human means. It is labour in vain to attempt it. It is our wisdom, therefore, not to irritate one another by opposition, but to derive every advantage we possibly can from a circumstance that will necessarily take place. There is as much diversity of sentiment, and consequent animosity in the church of England (as far as the members of it think for themselves at all) and even in the church of Rome, (notwithstanding the infallibility they pretend to in the decision of controversies) as among Dissenters, but without the advantage which they derive from their situation, of unconfined freedom of debate, and not having their inquiries restricted within certain limits only.

"We have now seen," says this author, p. 13. "on what principles the authority of a religious community, both over the ministers, and members of particular congregations, may be securely maintained, whether residing in the community at large, or delegated to some certain persons." We shall now examine in what manner he would join the authority of the civil magistrate to this system of church authority. Here, as he is wandering still farther from the simplicity of the gospel, we may naturally expect more wildness in his suppositions, and greater confusion in his reasoning.

"Because we see," says he, p. 14. "by the history of all ages, that religion, in the hands of selfish and factious men, is a very dangerous instrument; it, therefore, greatly concerns the public peace and safety, that all church authority should be under the control of the civil governor; that religious assemblies, as well as others, should be subject to his inspection, and bound by such rules as he shall see fit to impose. The most effectual method of obtaining this security, is to invest the supreme power, civil and ecclesiastical, in the same person. There are, indeed, good reasons why the offices of religion ought not to be administered by the magistrate. Both the education of his youth, and the attention of his riper years, have been employed on very different objects; and amidst the numberless toils and cares of government, it is impossible he should find leisure for any inferior profession."

P. 12. "To obtain completely the benefits proposed from this union of civil and ecclesiastical authority, all the members of the same community should be members also of the same church; variety of sects having a natural tendency both to weaken the influence of public religion, and to give disturbance to the public peace. Where this is impracticable, not the *best*, but the *largest* sect will naturally demand the protection of the magistrate."

P. 19. "As ministers, while employed by public authority, are not at liberty to depart from established forms, or to assemble separate congregations; so neither are the people at liberty, while they remain in society, to desert at pleasure, their lawful pastors, and flock in crowds to receive instruction from those who have no authority to give it. If they cannot lawfully comply with the terms of communion, let them make an open separation. In vain do men unite in civil or religious communities, if each individual is to retain intire liberty of judging and acting for himself."

Concerning the impropriety and absurdity of making a civil magistrate the supreme head of a christian church, I think enough has been advanced above. I should, indeed, have thought that the same reasons which this author gives, why the civil magistrate should not be concerned in the *offices* of religion, might have made him, at least, suspect his qualifications for super-intending the whole business of religion, and directing all the officers in it. According to this maxim, a person might be very fit for the office of a bishop, and especially an archbishop, who was by no means qualified to be a common curate. But to prevent disturbances, the civil magistrate must have security for the good behaviour of all his subjects, whatever be their religious persuasion; and, as he observes, the *most effectual* method (he does not say *the only sufficient* method, though it be precisely the thing that his argument requires) of obtaining this security is to invest the supreme power, civil and ecclesiastical, in the same person, be they ever so incompatible, and the same person ever so ill qualified to conduct them both.

But is not this, as I have hinted (in the parenthesis in the last paragraph) giving the civil magistrate much more power than, upon his own premises, is necessary? Is it not possible that all church-authority should be *sufficiently* under the control of the civil government, and that religious assemblies, as well as others, should be subject to his inspection, and even be bound by many of his rules, so far as was necessary to prevent any breach of the public peace, without investing him with supreme ecclesiastical power. For my own part, I should have no objection to the presence of an inspector from the civil magistrate in a religious assembly, or the attendance of as many constables, or even soldiers, as might be judged necessary to keep the peace, upon all occasions in which religion is concerned; and, if the civil magistrate be no more concerned in this business than the public peace and safety is concerned (and this writer himself does not so much as hint at any thing more) I should think this might satisfy him. But both he, and the civil magistrate want much more than this, when the latter must needs pass out of his proper character, and insist upon being the supreme head of the church. The avowed object and end of the union of civil and ecclesiastical power will not justify this claim, for it may be compassed at a much less expense. If I want a house that will not be blown down by the wind, and two feet of thickness in the wall will sufficiently answer my purpose, should I make it twenty feet thick, because this would be a *more effectual*, or the *most effectual* security? A *sufficient* security is enough for me.

The Doctor's reasoning in this case, is of a piece with the obligation which he lays upon the magistrate to countenance the *largest* sect of his discordant subjects, in preference to the *best*. This, indeed, might tend to reconcile the Dissenters in his dominions to their situation, by considering that their magistrate himself, the supreme head of the established church, could not command the religion of his choice any more than they could; for though he prescribed to one part of his subjects, the other part of them dictated to him; and that he was under the disagreeable necessity of enacting the articles of a religion which he himself did not believe.

The Bishop of Gloucester too, Dr Balguy's master in the science of defence, says, that "the state must make an alliance with the *largest* of the religious societies." I wish that either of these gentlemen, or any person for them, would tell us what ought to be the established religion of Ireland on these principles. Certainly, not that of the church of England; for, if I be rightly informed, there are many parishes in that kingdom, in which the clergy of the established church do no duty at all, because they can find none of their parishioners who would attend their ministrations. Had Constantine the Great been aware of the force of this reasoning, though a christian himself, he would have thought himself obliged to strengthen the establishment of the heathen worship, and to discountenance the profession of christianity in the Roman empire. For the same reason, also, a Protestant king of France would be obliged to continue the revocation of the edict of Nantz. It is really very difficult to animadvert upon such positions as these, and retain one's gravity at the same time.

There is something one cannot help smiling at in the reasons which Dr Balguy gives for the *legal maintenance* of christian ministers. "This provision," he says, p. 16. "is of great importance to them and the public, as we may easily judge from the wretched and precarious condition of those who want it; a condition which seldom fails to produce a slavish dependence, highly unbecoming a public teacher, and in some measure disqualifying him for the discharge of his office."

If our Lord had imagined that any real advantage would have accrued to the ministers of his gospel from a legal provision, I do not see why we might not (either in his discourses or parables) have expected some hint of it, and some recommendation of an alliance of his kingdom with those of this world, in order to secure it to them.

But no idea of such policy as this can be collected from the New Testament. For my part, I wonder how any man can read it, and retain the idea of any such worldly policy; so far am I from thinking it could have been collected from it.

Upon the whole, when I consider my situation as a minister of the gospel, or a member of a christian society, I do not see what either the state, or myself, could get by an *alliance*, admitting there was nothing unnatural, and absurd in the idea of such a connection. I want nothing that the state can give me (except to be unmolested by it) for I want neither a *legal maintenance*, nor *power to enforce my admonitions*. I look upon both these things as unsuitable to, and destructive of, the proper ends of my ministry. And, without any hire from the civil powers, I shall think it my duty to do all I can towards making my hearers good subjects, by making them good men, and good christians. I shall, therefore, never court any alliance with the state; and should the state be so absurd as to make any proposals of alliance with me, I hope I should have virtue enough to reject them with indignation, as Peter did the not very dissimilar offer of Simon Magus. Let the men of this world, and the powers of this world know, that there are some things that cannot be purchased with *money*.

In the same spirit are this writer's reasons for the difference of ranks among the clergy, and for a provision suitable to those ranks. "And will not the same reasons, p. 16. serve peculiarly to recommend those forms of government, in which the clergy, as well as the laity, are distributed into different ranks, and enabled to support those ranks in a becoming manner; that both the lower orders may avoid contempt, and the higher obtain distinction and regard? Were all the ministers placed in low stations of life, it is easy to see with what neglect they would be treated, and with what prejudice their doctrine would be received. Poverty, awkwardness, and ignorance of what is called the world, are disadvantages, for which the highest attainments in learning and virtue could never atone."

I shall close my remarks on this writer's method of defending the establishment, with repeating a trite observation, that there is, generally, both a *true*, and an *ostensible* reason for men's conduct, and that these are often very different from one another; because I cannot help thinking, that it is verified in the case before us. The ostensible, and plausible reasons for church establishments, are such as this writer has represented, derived from the imaginary evils attending the want of them; but the true reason with respect to the ministers, may be the scantiness and uncertainty of their provision without them; and, with respect to the civil magistrate, the vast addition of influence he thereby acquires, in consequence, both of having so many benefices at his disposal, and likewise, of retaining in his pay the public instructors of the people; men, who being kept in continual expectation, by the exhibition of higher preferment and greater emolument, will not fail to inculcate maxims the most favourable to the establishment, and increase of that power on which they depend.

But firm as the connection seems to be between the civil and ecclesiastical power, a connection cemented by *mutual worldly advantage*, this *high alliance* may yet be broken, and interest *divide* what interest has *united*. It has often seemed good to divine wisdom to *take the wise in their own craftiness*, and to bring about his own designs by the very means that were used to defeat them. Of this we have a recent example in France, in which we have seen the necessities of the state compelling its governors to abolish the richest of the religious orders. Did not the English ministry, who have not so large a *standing army* as the French, want more dependants of other kinds, so that *honours, pensions*, and *church preferments*, are extremely convenient to them, something similar to this might take place in England: and who can tell what may be the case, when some future tyrannical administration shall not be able to ride the storm they have raised, or to struggle, without unusual resources, with the difficulties in which they shall have involved themselves.

The remainder of the largest quotation I lately made from this writer, plainly respects the *Methodists*, at whose conduct he seems to have taken great offence. I agree with him, that *ministers*, while they are employed by public authority, are not at liberty to depart from established forms; but I can see no reason in the world why, in a country that admits of toleration, the *people* may not desert their usual places of public worship, and return to them whenever they please. Have the laity subscribed to any articles of faith, or formulary of religious worship? If not, they are clearly at liberty to act as they shall think most convenient, and to dissent partially or totally, secretly or openly, as they like best. But it is probable, that this author may not mean being at liberty with respect to the *laws of this country*, but with respect to *conscience*; so that though the law allows a man to quit the worship of the church of England, either occasionally or entirely, his conscience should dictate to him to do it intirely and wholly, if at all; which, to me, sounds strange and paradoxical enough.

The situation of conscientious laymen in the church of England, according to the casuistry of Dr Balguy, is truly remarkable, and such as, I dare say, few, or none of them are aware of. If they were, easily as the common people are generally led by the priests, I think the spirit of an *Englishman* would revolt at it. For this writer absolutely declares, that "the union of civil and ecclesiastical powers in the establishment is in vain, if each individual is to retain entire liberty of judging and acting for himself." Certainly a churchman ought to insist upon receiving some very great advantage in the establishment, as an equivalent for the surrender of this great and important natural right, *to judge and act for himself.* Upon the principles of this writer, a professed churchman is not at liberty so much as to hear a single sermon by those who have no legal authority to preach, *i.e. Dissenters* and *Methodists* (or, as he chooses to call them, *sectaries*, and *enthusiasts;*) so that he is cut off from the very means of judging for himself: for certainly this writer cannot have less objection to his parishioners *reading* the discourses of sectaries and Methodists, than to their *hearing* them.

This writer, indeed, is inconsistent enough to allow the members of the established church to make an *open* separation from it, if they cannot *lawfully* comply with the terms of communion. But were the terms ever so unlawful, what chance has any person for coming at the knowledge of it? Can it be supposed that a man should at once, of himself, and without any means of information, become so dissatisfied with the service of the church, that he should think it unlawful to join in it? I dare say the Doctor imagined no such event. But, in point of conscience, why may not a person think himself at liberty to leave the communion of the church, though he should not think it *unlawful.* May it not be sufficient that he thinks another form of religion *preferable* to it?

Take the whole paragraph that I have quoted, and I really think it a curiosity both in point of sentiment and reasoning; but, withal, one of the greatest insults that I have yet seen offered to the understandings and spirit of men. And yet this is from an Englishman, to Englishmen.

The Dissenters are obliged to this writer for the good-will he seems to bear them, in being an advocate for *toleration* in general; but I cannot help saying, I think him a very awkward, and inconsistent advocate in the case, and that intolerance would be much more agreeable to his general principles. If it be true, as he says, p. 17. that "a variety of sects has a natural tendency both to weaken the influence of public religion, and to give disturbance to the public peace," how is the magistrate "unqualified, or uncommissioned, to persecute for conscience sake?" Is he not constituted the guardian of the public peace, and must he not use the most effectual means to prevent the disturbance of it? If, "in order to obtain completely the benefits proposed from the union of civil and ecclesiastical authority, all the members of the same common-wealth should be members also of the same church," a conscientious civil magistrate might think it his duty, and well worth his while, to hazard something, with a prospect of insuring so great an advantage; especially as, according to this writer, it is only when the union of all the members of the commonwealth in one church is *impracticable*, that toleration is necessary. I own I should be very sorry to trust the civil magistrate with Dr Balguy's general maxims of civil and ecclesiastical policy. I would not even trust Dr Balguy himself in certain circumstances, when his principles give me so uncertain a hold of him. But toleration, very fortunately, happens to be the *fashionable* doctrine at present; and it must be incorporated into every system, how ill soever it may connect with it.

An example of one of the mischiefs attending establishments Dr Balguy has given in himself, in the conclusion of this sermon, in which he reflects very severely upon the author of the *Confessional*, and his friends; for I think it is very evident, that his censures respect nobody else. "There is," says this writer, p. 20. "one class of men, to whom this plea for compassion" (due to Methodists, as out of the reach of rational conviction) "will not extend. Those I mean who, without any pretence to inspiration, live in open war with the national church; with that very church of which they profess themselves minis-ters, and whose wages they continue to take, though in actual service against her. Whether this conduct proceed from a dislike to all establishments, or from a desire of erecting a new one, on the ruins of that which subsists at present, in either case, it is contrary to the most evident principles of justice and honour."

We see then, that when religion has once been established, all the ministers of it are to be considered as *servants in her pay*, and bound to fight for her and support her. The very *proposal* of a reformation by any member of an establishment, is contrary to the most evident principles of justice and honour; a maxim that shuts the door against all reformations that may not be called violent ones. Every disorder, how flagrant soever, must be winked at, so long as a person continues in the church; and in order to put himself into a situation to *propose* an amendment, he must quit his preferments, and declare war as an alien.. This sufficiently justifies the common complaint against establishments, that they never reform themselves, but that all reformations have ever been forced upon them *ab extra*. This has, hitherto, been matter of surprise to many persons, and some (among whom, I think, is the Bishop of Gloucester) have pretended to deny the charge, but now it appears to be rather a matter of boasting; for it would have been contrary to the most evident principles of justice and honour, for the clergy to have made the attempt.

It is not improbable, but that Dr Balguy and his friends, if they would explain themselves freely, might carry this *point of honour* a little farther, and say, that no person who has ever *eaten the bread*, or *tasted the salt* of the church, should lift up his heel against her; nor perhaps the man whose father, or grandfather had eaten of it.

I should think the most scrupulous casuist might allow a clergyman, who is dissatisfied with the church, to make a fair attempt to procure the reformation of those abuses that are intolerable to him; and, consequently, to wait a proper time, to see the effect of his endeavours, before he absolutely quitted his station in the church. For if his endeavours succeed, he will have no occasion to quit it at all; and, in the mean time, the remonstrances of a person who is a member of the church, may be expected to have a more favourable hearing, than those of one who has no connection with it.

So far am I from joining with Dr Balguy, in his harsh censures of the author of the *Confessional*, that I rather think that every principle of justice and honour should prompt a man to use his best endeavours for the benefit of any community of which he is a member, and of whose privileges he partakes. If, therefore, there be any thing wrong in the constitution of it, those principles require him to promote a reformation of the abuse; and it would be manifestly contrary to the principles of justice and honour, to be an unconcerned spectator of so great a misfortune to it. I cannot help comparing the author of the *Confessional* to a man who would endeavour to stop a leak he perceived in the vessel in which he was embarked, and Dr Balguy to a man who would run the risk of its sinking all at once, rather than insinuate that there was any thing amiss with it.

Strange as this author's declamation against the friends of the *Confessional* is, it follows directly from his avowed principle, that *authority once established must be obeyed.* Speaking of "the founders of our holy religion," he says, p. 18. "They established a form of church government; for the church *must* be governed in *some* form, or there could be *no* government. But their directions to us are, for the most part, very general. Even their example must be cautiously urged, in different times, and under different circumstances. In this one point they are clear and explicit, that authority *once established* must be *obeyed.*"

But was not popery *once established* in this island? How then is it possible, upon these principles of *passive obedience* and *non-resistance*, to vindicate the reformation? Whatever it be that is once established, and in whatever manner it is once established, it must, it seems, be submitted to. If this principle be applied without restriction, it will vindicate the continuance of every system, the most absurd and mischievous in the world; and if it do admit of restriction and limitation, it could signify nothing to this author's purpose to allege it.

It might have been expected, that a writer who is so extremely severe upon those who propose a reformation in the church, while they continue in it, should have expressed some degree of indignation against those who intrude themselves into it by *false oaths* and pretences, subscribing the articles and canons, &c. when they disbelieve and ridicule them. But I fancy that I can put my reader into possession of the *secret reason*, why nothing of this kind occurs in the writings of the friends of church authority. Men who have come *this way* into the church have always proved its firmest friends. Having made no bones of their own scruples, they pay no regard to the scruples of others. A conscientious bigot to the church is not half so much to be depended upon, as the man who believes not a single word of the matter, nor is he so fit to be admitted into the cabinet council of church-power.

Such, my gentle reader, are the maxims, and such the reasoning with which this writer stands forth to support the declining cause of church-authority. For he justly complains, p. 5. that "notwithstanding the members of the church of England have, from its foundation, been carefully instructed in these points, by its ablest defenders, yet, so capricious is the public taste, that these great writers have gradually fallen into neglect. Their doctrines are now, in a manner, forgotten, and enthusiasts and sectaries revive the same follies, and defend them by the same arguments, which were once effectually overthrown." In this deplorable situation of things, this great champion has judged it "not to be improper to resume the beaten subject, and to explain, on rational principles, the foundation of church authority."

It is, indeed, truly deplorable, that these *great authors* should have fallen into neglect, and that their excellent doctrines should be, in a manner, forgotten; but this misfortune has been owing, chiefly, to themselves. The truth is, that these great writers have been very inconsistent with one another, which is a very unfavourable and suspicious circumstance for the cause they are so zealously labouring to support. While each of them is busily pursuing his own separate scheme, and they are applying their very different methods to gain the same end, they only obstruct and embarrass one another.

In reality, the principles of the Dissenters are not more opposite, either to those of Hooker or Warburton, than those of these two great champions for church-authority are to one another; and other writers have proposed other schemes of church power quite different from them both. Now if three persons be building a house, and one of them will have it of brick, another of stone, and the third of wood; and if each be so obstinate, that he will pull down what the others build, how can it be expected that the edifice should be completed? or how can the spectators refrain from laughing to see them so laboriously employed? If I may be indulged another comparison, I would say, that when the schemes of the different writers, in defence of ecclesiastical establishments, are considered together, they make such kind of harmony, as would result from a number of persons singing the same words, each to his own favourite tune, at the same time.

In these circumstances, I cannot help thinking that Dr Balguy is unreasonably severe upon the members of his own church, and expects too much from them, when he says, p. 4. "It might well have been expected, that the members of the English church should have seen farther, and judged better (than to *consult the scriptures for what is not to be found in it*, with respect to church government) because this church, even from its foundation, has been carefully instructed on these very points by some of its ablest defenders. But so capricious is the public taste," &c. Had these *ablest defenders* of the church defended her upon the *same principles*, and upon the same general maxims of church power, this writer's censures might have been just; for, by a proper degree of attention and deference to such *instructors*, they might have been long ago well grounded in this important branch of knowledge. But he only says that *some of the ablest defenders* of the church, not *all* of them have instructed her so carefully. And were the members of the church ever so desirous of receiving instruction, either for their own benefit, or that of their teachers, what proficiency could they be expected to make, when their *ablest masters* did not teach the same general doctrines?

If this hath been the case, even from the foundation of this church (which, in proportion to its occasions, has been blest with so many able defenders) how much more embarrassed must her members have been since the publication of the *Confessional*, when (if I be rightly informed, for I have not yet read any of them myself) almost every oppugner of that excellent work has adopted a different system of church-authority; so that, as the controversy proceeds, we may expect to be entertained with the exhibition of as many crude systems of church power, as there are said to have been *unformed animals* in Egypt, after an inundation of the Nile. I do not know what we should do after such another inundation, but that these half-formed beings generally perish as soon as they have shown any signs of life.

Since, however, the ablest defenders of the church *will*, each, go their own way to work, suppose that, in order to make the best of this unfavourable circumstance, those who are to be instructed by these able masters be distributed into *distinct classes*, and that care be taken, that they do not intermix with one another. Provided the same *end* be answered, and the church be supported, what doth it signify how different, or inconsistent are the means by which it is effected? When this experiment has been made, that mode of instruction may be adopted, in exclusion of the rest, which shall be found in fact, to make the most zealous churchmen. In the issue, I suspect, that though the *modern improvements* in the science of church government may appear to be the best for the politer and more free-thinking part of the nation, nothing will be found to answer so well with the common people, who do not easily enter into refinements, as the old-fashioned *jure divino* doctrines. I am afraid Dr Warburton has been rather impolitic in decrying those *old supports* of the cause, rotten as he thinks them to be. They have been of excellent service in their day.

To conclude this section with perfect seriousness. I congratulate my reader, and the age in which we live, that the *great writers* (as Dr Balguy calls them) in defence of church power, have fallen into neglect, and that their doctrines are, in a manner, forgotten. To account for this remarkable fact, in an age, in which knowledge of all other kinds (and especially the knowledge of *government* and *laws*, and I think the knowledge of *religion* too) has been so greatly advanced, may surprise the Doctor and his friends, and therefore they may resolve it into *caprice* or *chance*; but it is no surprise to me, or my friends. *Magna est veritas, &c.*[37] the translation of which saying I shall give my reader in the words of this author, p. 9. "Truth can never suffer from a free inquiry. The combat may be sharp, but she is sure to conquer in the end." And though the performance I am animadverting upon be an attempt to revive the memory of some of the arguments in defence of church-authority, I trust it will only serve to hold them forth once more to the generous contempt and detestation of men of sense and reflection; and accelerate their being finally consigned to everlasting oblivion, as the disgrace of human reason, and human nature.

SECTION X.

Of the Progress of Civil Societies to a State of greater Perfection, showing that it is retarded by Encroachments on Civil and Religious Liberty.

The great argument in favour of the perpetuation of ecclesiastical establishments is, that as they suit the several forms of civil government under which they have taken place, the one cannot be touched

---

[37] 'Great is truth and it will triumph' (4 Esdras 4: 41).

without endangering the other. I am not insensible of the truth there is in the principle on which this apprehension is grounded; but I think the connection (artfully as those things have been interwoven) is not so strict, but that they may be separated, at least, in a course of time. But allowing that some change might take place in our civil constitution, in consequence of the abolition, or reformation of the ecclesiastical part, it is more than an equal chance, that the alteration will be for the better; and no real friend to his country can wish to perpetuate its present constitution in church or state, so far as to interrupt its progress to greater perfection than it has yet attained to.

I can heartily join with the greatest admirers of the English constitution, in their encomiums upon it, when it is compared with that of any other country in the world. I really think it to be the best actual scheme of civil policy; but if any person should say, that it is perfect, and that no alteration can be made in it for the better, I beg leave to withhold my assent. Dr Brown himself doth not hesitate to acknowledge, that there are imperfections in it. How then can a real friend to his country wish to fix its imperfections upon it, and make them perpetual?

It will be said, that alterations may, indeed, be made, but cannot be made with safety, and without the danger of throwing every thing into confusion; so that, upon the whole, things had better remain as they are: but, allowing this, for the present, why should they be *perpetuated* as they are? If the proposed alterations were *violent* ones, that is, introduced by violent measures, they might justly give alarm to all good citizens. I would endeavour to stop the ablest hand that should attempt to reform in this manner; because it is hardly possible but that a remedy so effected must be worse than the disease. But still, why should we object to any state's gradually reforming itself, or throw obstacles in the way of such reformations?

All civil societies, and the whole science of civil government, on which they are founded, are yet in their infancy. Like other arts and sciences, this is gradually improving; but it improves more slowly, because opportunities for making experiments are fewer. Indeed, hardly any trials in legislation have ever been made by persons who had knowledge and ability to collect from history, and to compare the observations which might be of use for this purpose, or had leisure to digest them properly at the time. Taking it for granted, therefore, that our constitution and laws have not escaped the imperfections which we see to be incident to every thing human; by all means, let the closest attention be given to them, let their excellencies and defects be thoroughly laid open, and let improvements of every kind be made; but not such as would prevent all farther improvements: because it is not probable, that any improvements, which the utmost sagacity of man could now suggest, would be an equivalent for the prevention of all that might be made hereafter. Were the best formed state in the world to be fixed in its present condition, I make no doubt but that, in a course of time, it would be the worst.

History demonstrates this truth with respect to all the celebrated states of antiquity; and as all things (and particularly whatever depends upon science) have of late years been in a quicker progress towards perfection than ever; we may safely conclude the same with respect to any political state now in being. What advantage did Sparta (the constitution of whose government was so much admired by the ancients, and many moderns) reap from those institutions which contributed to its longevity, but the longer continuance of, what I should not scruple to call, the worst government we read of in the world; a government which secured to a man the fewest of his natural rights, and of which a man who had a taste for life would least of all choose to be a member. While the arts of life were improving in all the neighbouring nations, Sparta derived this noble prerogative from her constitution, that she continued the nearest to her pristine barbarity; and in the space of near a thousand years (which includes the whole period in which letters and the arts were the most cultivated in the rest of Greece) produced no one poet, orator, historian, or artist of any kind. The convulsions of Athens, where life was in some measure enjoyed, and the faculties of body and mind had their proper exercise and gratification, were, in my opinion, far preferable to the savage uniformity of Sparta.

The constitution of Egypt was similar to that of Sparta, and the advantages that country received from it were similar. Egypt was the mother of the arts to the states of Greece; but the rigid institutions of this mother of the arts kept them in their infancy; so that the states of Greece, being more favourably situated for improvements of all kinds, soon went beyond their instructress; and no improvements of any kind were ever made in Egypt, till it was subdued by a foreign power. What would have been the state of agriculture, ship-building, or war, if those arts had been fixed in England two or three centuries ago?

Dr Brown will urge me with the authority of Plutarch, who largely extols the regulations of Egypt and of Sparta, and censures the Roman legislators for adopting nothing similar to them. But I beg leave to appeal from the authority of Plutarch, and of all the ancients, as by no means competent judges in this case. Imperfect as the science of government is at present, it is certainly much more perfect than it was in their time. On the authority of the ancients, Dr Brown might as well contend for another institution of the famed Egyptians; viz. their obliging all persons to follow the occupations of their fathers; and perhaps this might be no bad auxiliary to his prescribed mode of education, and prevent the springing up of faction in a state. It would likewise favour another object, which the doctor has professedly in view, viz. checking the growth of commerce.

Supposing this wise system of perpetuation had occurred to our ancestors in the feudal times, and that an assembly of old English barons, with their heads full of their feudal rights and services, had imitated the wise Spartans, and perpetuated the severe feudal institutions; what would England at this day have been (with the unrivalled reputation of uniformity and constancy in its laws) but the most barbarous, the weakest, and most distracted state in Europe? It is plain from fact, that divine providence had greater things in view in favour of these kingdoms; and has been conducting them through a series of gradual changes (arising from internal and external causes) which have brought us to our present happy condition; and which, if suffered to go on, may carry us to a pitch of happiness of which we can yet form no conception.

Had the religious system of our oldest forefathers been established on these wise and perpetual foundations, we had now been pagans, and our priests druids. Had our Saxon conquerors been endued with the same wisdom and foresight, we had been worshipping Thor and Woden; and had our ancestors, three centuries ago, persevered in this spirit, we had been blind and priest-ridden papists. The greatest blessing that can befall a state, which is so rigid and inflexible in its institutions, is to be conquered by a people, who have a better government, and have made farther advances in the arts of life. And it is undoubtedly a great advantage which the divine being has provided for this world, that conquests and revolutions should give mankind those opportunities of reforming their systems of government, and of improving the science of it, which they would never have found themselves.

In the excellent constitution of nature, evils of all kinds, some way or other, find their proper remedy; and when government, religion, education, and every thing that is valuable in society seems to be in so fine a progress towards a more perfect state, is it not our wisdom to favour this progress; and to allow the remedies of all disorders to operate gradually and easily, rather than, by a violent system of perpetuation, to retain all disorders till they force a remedy? In the excellent constitution of the human body, a variety of outlets are provided for noxious humours, by means of which the system relieves itself when any slight disorders happen to it. But, if these outlets be obstructed, the whole system is endangered by the convulsions which ensue.

Some things in civil society do, in their own nature, require to be established, or fixed by law for a considerable time; but that part of the system, for the reasons mentioned above, will certainly be the most imperfect; and therefore it is the wisdom of the legislature to make that part as small as possible, and to let the establishments, which are necessary, be as easy as is consistent with the tolerable order of society. It is an universal maxim, that the more liberty is given to every thing which is in a state of growth, the more perfect it will become; and when it is grown to its full size, the more amply will it repay its wise parent, for the indulgence given to it in its infant state. A judicious father will bear with the forwardness of his children, and overlook many slights of youth; which can give him no pleasure, but from the prospect they afford of his children becoming useful and valuable men, when the fire of youth is abated.

I do not pretend to define what degree of establishment is necessary for many things relating to civil society: but thus much I think is clear, that every system of policy is too strict and violent, in which any thing that may be the instrument of general happiness, is under so much restraint, that it can never reform itself from the disorders which may be incident to it; when it is so circumstanced, that it cannot improve as far as it is capable of improvement, but that every reformation must necessarily be introduced from some other quarter; in which case it must generally be brought about by force. Is it not a standing argument that religion, in particular, has been too much confined, in all countries, that the body of the clergy have never reformed themselves; and that all reformations have ever been forced upon them, and have generally been attended with the most horrible persecutions, and dangerous convulsions in the state? I cannot help thinking also, that every system of government is violent and tyrannical, which incapacitates men of the best abilities, and of the greatest integrity, from rendering their country any service in their power, while those who pay no regard to conscience may have free access to all places of power and profit.

It seems to be the uniform intention of divine providence, to lead mankind to happiness in a progressive, which is the surest, though the slowest method. Evil always leads to good, and imperfect to perfect. The divine being might, no doubt, have adopted a different plan, have made human nature and human governments perfect from the beginning. He might have formed the human mind with an intuitive knowledge of truth, without leading men through so many labyrinths of error. He might have made man perfectly virtuous, without giving so much exercise to his passions in his struggles with the habits of vice. He might have sent an angel, or have commissioned a man to establish a perfect form of civil government; and, *a priori*, this would seem to have been almost as essential to human happiness as any system of truth; at least, that it would have been a valuable addition to a system of religious truth: but though it would be impiety in us to pretend to fathom the depths of the divine councils, I think we may fairly conclude, that if this method of proceeding had been the best for us, he, whom we cannot conceive to be influenced by any thing but his desire to promote the happiness of his creatures, would have pursued it. But a contrary method has been adopted in every thing relating to us.

How many falls does a child get before it learns to walk secure. How many inarticulate sounds precede those which are articulate. How often are we imposed upon by all our senses before we learn to form a right judgment of the proper objects of them. How often do our passions mislead us, and involve us in difficulties, before we reap the advantage they were intended to bring us in our pursuit of happiness; and how many false judgments do we make, in the investigation of all kinds of truth, before we come to a right conclusion. How many ages do errors and prejudices of all kinds prevail, before they are dissipated by the light of truth, and how general, and how long was the reign of false religion before the propagation of the true! How late was christianity, that great remedy of vice and ignorance, introduced! How slow and how confined its progress!

In short, it seems to have been the intention of divine providence, that mankind should be, as far as possible, *self taught*; that we should attain to every thing excellent and useful, as the result of our own experience and observation; that our judgments should be formed by the appearances which are presented to them, and our hearts instructed by their own feelings. But by the unnatural system of rigid unalterable establishments, we put it out of our power to instruct ourselves, or to derive any advantage from the lights we acquire from experience and observation; and thereby, as far as is in our power, we counteract the kind intentions of the deity in the constitution of the world, and in providing for a state of constant, though slow improvement in every thing.

A variety of useful lessons may be learned from our attention to the conduct of divine providence respecting us. When history and experience demonstrate the uniform method of divine providence to have been what has been above represented, let us learn from it to be content with the natural, though slow progress we are in to a more perfect state. But let us always endeavour to keep things in this progress. Let us, however, beware, lest by attempting to accelerate, we in fact retard our progress in happiness. But more especially, let us take heed, lest, by endeavouring to secure and perpetuate the great ends of society, we in fact defeat those ends. We shall have a thousand times more enjoyment of a happy and perfect form of government, when we can see in history the long progress of our constitution through barbarous and imperfect systems of policy; as we are more confirmed in the truth, and have more enjoyment of it, by reviewing the many errors by which we were misled in our pursuit of it. If the divine being saw that the best form of government, that even he could have prescribed for us, would not have answered the end of its institution, if it had been imposed by himself; much less can we imagine it could answer any valuable purpose, to have the crude systems (for they can be nothing more) of short-sighted men for ever imposed upon us.

Establishments, be they ever so excellent, still fix things somewhere; and this circumstance, which is all that is pleaded for them amounts to, is with me the greatest objection to them. I wish to see things *in a progress* to a better state, and no obstructions thrown in the way of reformation.

In spite of all the fetters we can lay upon the human mind, notwithstanding all possible discouragements in the way of free inquiry, knowledge of all kinds, and religious knowledge among the rest, will increase. The wisdom of one generation will ever be folly in the next. And yet, though we have seen this verified in the history of near two thousand years, we persist in the absurd maxim of making a preceding generation dictate to a succeeding one, which is the same thing as making the foolish instruct the wise; for what is a lower degree of wisdom but comparative folly?

Had even Locke, Clarke, Hoadley, and others, who have gained immortal reputation by their freedom of thinking, but about half a century ago, been appointed to draw up a creed, they would have inserted in it such articles of faith, as myself, and hundreds more, should now think unscriptural, and absurd: nay, articles, which they would have thought of great importance, we should think conveyed a reflection upon the moral government of God, and were injurious to virtue among men. And can we think that wisdom will die with us! No, our creeds, could we be so inconsistent with ourselves as to draw up any, would, I make no doubt, be rejected with equal disdain by our posterity.

That ecclesiastical establishments have really retarded the reformation from popery is evident from the face of things in Europe. Can it be thought that all the errors and abuses which had been accumulating in the space of fifteen hundred years, should be rectified in less than fifty, by men educated with strong prejudices in favour of them all? and yet the Augsburg confession, I believe, stands unrepealed; the church of England is the same now that it was in the reign of Queen Elizabeth; and the church of Scotland is to this day in that imperfect and crude state in which *John Knox* left it.

Little did those great reformers, whose memory I revere, think what burdens they, who had boldly shaken off the load from their own shoulders, were laying on those of others; and that the moment they had nobly freed themselves from the yoke of servitude, they were signing an act to enslave all that should come after them; forgetting the golden rule of the gospel, to do to others as we would that they should do to us.

Could religious knowledge have remained in the state in which the first reformers left it; could the stone they had once moved from its seat, on the top of a precipice, have been stopped in its course, their provisions for perpetuation would have been wise and excellent; but their eyes were hardly closed, before their children found that their fathers had been too precipitate. They found their own hands tied up by their unthinking parents, and the knots too many, and too tight for them to unloose.

The great misfortune is, that the progress of knowledge is chiefly among the thinking few. The bulk of mankind being educated in a reverence for established modes of thinking and acting, in consequence of their being established, will not hear of a reformation proceeding even so far as they could really wish, lest, in time, it should go farther than they could wish, and the end be worse than the beginning. And where there are great emoluments in a church, it is possessed of the strongest internal guard against all innovations whatever. Church livings must not be touched, and they may, if any thing else be meddled with. This makes the situation of sensible and conscientious men, in all establishments, truly deplorable. Before I had read that excellent work, intitled the *Confessional*, but much more since, it has grieved me to see the miserable shifts that such persons (whether in the church of England, or of Scotland) are obliged to have recourse to, in order to gild the pill, which they must swallow or starve; and to observe their poor contrivances to conceal the chains that gall them. But it grieves one no less, to see the rest of their brethren, hugging their chains and proud of them.

But let those gentlemen in the church, who oppose every step towards reformation, take care, lest they overact their parts, and lest some enterprizing persons, finding themselves unable to *untie* the Gordian knots of authority, should, like another Alexander the Great, boldly *cut* them all. Let them take care, lest, for want of permitting a few repairs in their ruinous house, it should at last fall all together about their ears. A number of spirited and conscientious men, openly refusing to enter into the church, or throwing up the livings which they hold upon those iniquitous and enslaving terms (and such men there have been in this country) would rouse the attention of the temporal heads of the spiritual part of our constitution. They would see the necessity of an immediate and complete reformation; and then the alarm of churchmen, with their paltry expedients and compromises, would come too late. The temper of these times would not bear another St Bartholomew.[38]

[If only *one or two* persons, of known probity and good sense, did now and then, act this heroic part, it would serve to keep up an attention to the subject. If *every man* who doth not in his conscience believe the articles he has subscribed, would magnanimously throw up the emoluments he enjoys in consequence of his subscription, it can hardly be doubted, but that a reformation of, at least, the capital abuses in the ecclesiastical system would take place the very next session of parliament. This nation would never suffer all her pulpits to be filled by such clergymen, as would then remain in the church.]

In the mean time, let the friends of liberty by no means give way to impatience. The longer it may be before this reformation takes place, the more *effectual* it will probably be. The times may not yet be ripe for such an one as you would wish to acquiesce in, considering that, whenever it is made, it will probably continue as long as the last has done.

It was well for the cause of truth and liberty, that the Romish clergy at the beginning of the reformation, held out with so much obstinacy against the smallest concessions; for had they but granted the cup to the laity, and been a little more decent in the article of indulgences, the rest of popery might have continued

"To scourge mankind for ten dark ages more."

And at the restoration here in England, had a few, a very few trifling alterations been complied with, such numbers of the Presbyterians would have heartily united to the established church, as would have enabled it entirely to crush every other sect, to prevent the growing liberty of the press, and to have maintained for ages the most rigid uniformity. This observation may, perhaps, teach patience to one party, and prudence to the other.

Dissenters, even of the presbyterian persuasion, have, by no means, been free from the general infatuation of other reformers. All the

---

[38] The St Bartholomew's Day Massacre (24 August 1572) began as an assassination of the Protestant leader Admiral Coligny and spread into a general Parisian – and later national – slaughter of Protestants.

denominations of dissenters have made attempts to fix things by their own narrow standard; and prescribed confessions of faith, even with subscriptions, have been introduced among them. But happily for us, there have always been men of generous and enlarged minds, who, having no civil power to contend with, have had courage to stem the torrent; and now, among those who are called the more *rational* part of the dissenters, things are not, upon the whole, to be complained of. No subscriptions to any articles of faith, or even to the new testament, is now required; and ministers are excused, if they choose not to give any confession of their own. To have preached and behaved like a christian, is deemed sufficient to recommend a man to the christian ministry. Unfettered by authority, they can pursue the most liberal plans of education. The whole business is to give the faculties of the mind their free play, and to point out proper objects of attention to students, without any concern what may be the result of their inquiries; the design being to make wise and useful men, and not the tools and abetters of any particular party.

If any person should think that religion is not to be put upon the same footing with other branches of knowledge (which they allow to require the aid of every circumstance favourable to their future growth) that since the whole of christianity was delivered at once, and is contained in the books of the new testament, there is no reason to expect more light than we already have with regard to it; and, therefore, that they are justified in fixing the knowledge of it where it *now* stands, I shall only say, that I sincerely pity their weakness and prejudice; as such an opinion can only proceed from a total ignorance of what has passed in the christian world, or from a bigotted attachment to the authoritative institutions of fallible men.

To recur to Dr Brown; he would raise the terms on which we are to live in society; so that, under his administration, a man could enjoy little more than bare security in the possession of his property, and that upon very hard conditions. The care he would take to shackle men's minds, in the first formation of their thinking powers, and to check their exertions when they were formed, would, I apprehend, put an effectual stop to all the noble improvements of which society is capable. Knowledge, particularly of the more sublime kinds, in the sciences of morals and religion, could expect no encouragement. He would have more restrictions laid upon the publication of books. He complains, p. 103, that, in the late reign, deistical publications proceeded almost without cognisance from the civil magistrate; and asserts (Appendix, p. 29) that there are *many* opinions or principles tending evidently to the destruction of society or freedom, and which, therefore, ought not to be tolerated in a well ordered free community.

The civil magistrate then, according to this writer, ought to control the press, and therefore prevent, by means of effectual penalties (or else he doth nothing) the publication of any thing, that might directly or indirectly, thwart his views of civil policy; which, in England, comprehends the present form of our established religion. But so extensive is the connection of all kinds of truth, that if a man would keep effectually clear of the subject of religion, he must not indulge a free range of thought near the confines of it. The subjects of metaphysics, morals, and natural religion would be highly dangerous. There might be heresy, or the foundation of heresy, without coming near revelation, or any of the peculiar doctrines of christianity. We must only be allowed to *think* for ourselves, without having the liberty of divulging, or, in any form, publishing our thoughts to others, not even to our children. A mighty privilege indeed! and for which we might think ourselves obliged to Dr Brown, if it were in the power of man to deprive us of it. This is a privilege which the poor wretch enjoys who lives under the same roof with a Spanish inquisitor. Even the subjects of the grand seignior enjoy far greater privileges than those which Dr Brown would indulge to Englishmen. For the greater part of them are allowed to educate their children in a religion, which teaches them to regard Mohammed as an impostor. Nay, the pope himself permits those to live unmolested, and under his protection at Rome, who look upon that church, of which he calls himself the head, as founded on fraud and falsehood, and to educate their children in the same principles. Nor hath the pope, or the grand seignior, ever seen reason to repent of their indulgence.

Were any more laws restraining the liberty of the press in force, it is impossible to say how far they might be construed to extend. Those already in being are more than are requisite, and inconsistent with the interests of truth. Were they to extend farther, every author would lie at the mercy of the ministers of state, who might condemn indiscriminately, upon some pretence or other, every work that gave them umbrage; under which circumstances might fall some of the greatest and noblest productions of the human mind, if such works could be produced in those circumstances. For if men of genius knew they could not publish the discoveries they made, they could not give free scope to their faculties in making and pursuing those discoveries. It is the thought of publication, and the prospect of fame which is, generally, the great incentive to men of genius to exert their faculties, in attempting the untrodden paths of speculation.

In those unhappy circumstances, writers would entertain a dread of every new subject. No man could safely indulge himself in any thing bold, enterprizing, and out of the vulgar road; and in all publications we should see a *timidity* incompatible with the spirit of discovery. If any towering genius should arise in those unfavourable circumstances, a Newton in the natural world, or a Locke, a Hutcheson, a Clarke, or a Hartley in the moral, the only effectual method to prevent their diffusing a spirit of enterprise and innovation, which is natural to such great souls, could be no other than that which Tarquin so significantly expressed, by taking off the heads of all those poppies which overlooked the rest. Such men could not but be dangerous, and give umbrage in a country where it was the maxim of the government, that every thing of importance should for ever remain unalterably fixed.

The whole of this system of uniformity appears to me to be founded on very narrow and short-sighted views of policy. A man of extensive views will overlook temporary evils, with a prospect of the greater good which may often result from, or be inseparably connected with them. He will bear with a few tares, lest, in attempting to root them out, he endanger rooting up the wheat with them. Unbounded free enquiry upon all kinds of subjects may certainly be attended with some inconvenience, but it cannot be restrained without infinitely greater inconvenience. The deistical performances Dr Brown is so much offended at may have unsettled the minds of some people, but the minds of many have been more firmly settled, and upon better foundations than ever. The scheme of christianity has been far better understood, since those deistical writings have occasioned the subject to be more thoroughly discussed than it had been before.

Besides, if truth stand upon the false foundation of prejudice or error, it is an advantage to it to be unsettled; and the man who doth no more, and even means to do no more, is, in fact, its friend. Another person seeing its destitute and baseless condition, may be induced to set it upon its proper foundation. Far better policy would it be to remove the difficulties which still lie in the way of free enquiry, than to throw fresh ones into it. Infidels would then be deprived of their most successful method of attacking christianity, namely, insinuation; and christian divines might, with a more manly grace, engage with the champions of deism, and in fact engage with more advantage, when they both fought on the same equal ground. As things are at present, I should be ashamed to fight under the shelter of the civil power, while I saw my adversary exposed to all the severity of it.

To the same purpose, I cannot help quoting the authority of Dr Warburton, "Nor less friendly is this liberty to the generous advocate of religion. For how could such an one, when in earnest convinced of the strength of evidence in his cause, desire an adversary whom the laws had before disarmed, or value a victory where the magistrate must triumph with him? even I, the meanest in this controversy, should have been ashamed of projecting the defence of the great Jewish legislator, did not I know, that his assailants and defenders skirmished under one equal law of liberty. And if my dissenting, in the course of this defence, from some common opinions needs an apology, I should desire it may be thought, that I ventured into this train with greater confidence, that I might show, by not intrenching myself in authorized speculations, I put myself upon the same footing with you [the deists] and would claim no privilege that was not enjoyed in common." Divine Legation, p. 7.

But sorry I am, that the paragraph which immediately follows, how proper soever it might be when it was written, looks like a tantalizing of his unfortunate adversaries. "This liberty, then, may you long possess, know how to use, and gratefully to acknowledge it. I say this, because one cannot, without indignation, observe, that, amidst the full enjoyment of it, you still continue, with the meanest affectation, to fill your prefaces with repeated clamours against the difficulties and discouragements attending the exercise of free thinking; and in a peculiar strain of modesty and reasoning, make use of this very liberty to persuade the world you still want it. In extolling liberty we can join with you, in the vanity of pretending to have contributed most to its establishment we can bear with you, but in the low cunning of pretending still to lie under restraints, we can neither join nor bear with you. There was, indeed, a time, and that within our memories, when such complaints were seasonable, and meritorious; but, happy for you gentlemen, you have outlived it. All the rest is merely sir

Martin, it is continuing to fumble at the lute though the music has been long over."

Let Peter Annet* (if he dare) write a comment on this passage. So far are deists from having free liberty to publish their sentiments, that even many christians cannot speak out with safety. In present circumstances, every christian divine is not at liberty to make use of those arguments which, he may think, would supply the best defence of christianity. What are, in the opinion of many, the very foundations of our faith, are in a ruinous condition, and must be repaired before it will be to any purpose to beautify and adorn the superstructure; but the man who should have the true courage and judgement, to go near enough to such rotten foundations, would be thought to mean nothing less than to undermine them, and intirely destroy the whole fabric. His very brethren would stand off from him, thinking him in league with their adversaries; and, by an ill judging zeal, might call in the destructive aid of the civil power to stop his hand. In consequence of which, notwithstanding his most laudable zeal in favour of our holy religion, he might stand upon the same pillory, and be thrown into the same prison with wretched and harmless infidels. Many undoubted friends of christianity, and men of the most enlarged minds, will know and feel what I mean.

Hitherto, indeed, few of the friends of free inquiry among christians have been more than partial advocates for it. If they find themselves under any difficulty with respect to their own sentiments, they complain, and plead strongly for the rights of conscience, of private judgement, and of free inquiry; but when they have gotten room enough for themselves, they are quite easy, and in no pain for others. The papist must have liberty to write against Pagans, Mohammedans, and Jews; but he cannot bear with protestants. Writers in defence of the church of England justify their separation from the church of Rome, but, with the most glaring inconsistency, call the protestant dissenters, schismatics; and many dissenters, forgetting the fundamental principles of their dissent, which are the same that are asserted by all christians and protestants in similar circumstances, discourage every degree of liberty greater than they themselves have

---

*Written in 1765, when that unfortunate man was just come out of Bridewell, where he had suffered a year's imprisonment and hard labour, for making some free remarks on the books of Moses.

taken, and have as great an aversion to those whom they are pleased to call heretics, as papists have for protestants, or as Laud had for the old puritans.

But why should we confine our neighbour, who may want more room, in the same narrow limits with ourselves. The wider we make the common circle of liberty, the more of its friends will it receive, and the stronger will be the common interest. Whatever be the particular views of the numerous tribes of searchers after truth, under whatever denomination we may be ranked; whether we be called, or call ourselves christians, papists, protestants, dissenters, heretics, or even deists (for all are equal here, all are actuated by the same spirit, and all engaged in the same cause) we stand in need of the same liberty of thinking, debating, and publishing. Let us, then, as far as our interest is the same, with one heart and voice, stand up for it. Not one of us can hurt his neighbour, without using a weapon which, in the hand of power, might as well serve to chastise himself. The present state of the English government (including both the laws, and the administration, which often corrects the rigour of the law) may, perhaps, bear my own opinions without taking much umbrage; but I could wish to congratulate many of my brother free-thinkers, on the greater indulgence which their more heretical sentiments may require.

To the honour of the Quakers be it spoken, that they are the only body of christians who have uniformly maintained the principles of christian liberty, and toleration. Every other body of men have turned persecutors when they had power. Papists have persecuted the protestants, the church of England has persecuted the dissenters, and other dissenters, in losing their name, lost that spirit of christian charity, which seemed to be essential to them. Short was their sunshine of power, and thankful may Britain, and the present dissenters be, that it was so. But the Quakers, though established in Pennsylvania, have persecuted none. This glorious principle seems so intimately connected with the fundamental maxims of their sect, that it may be fairly presumed, the moderation they have hitherto shown is not to be ascribed to the smallness of their party, or to their fear of reprisals. For this reason, if I were to pray for the general prevalence of any one sect of christians (which I should not think it for the interest of christianity to take place, even though I should settle the articles of it myself) it should be that of the Quakers; because, different as my opinions are from theirs, I have so much confidence in their moderation, that I believe they would let me live, write, and publish what I pleased unmolested among them. And this I own, is more than I could promise myself from any other body of christians whatever; the presbyterians by no means excepted.

The object of this forced uniformity is narrow and illiberal, unworthy of human nature. Supposing it accomplished, what is it possible to gain by it, but, perhaps, a more obstinate and blind belief in the vulgar; while men of sense, seeing themselves debarred the very means of conviction, must of course be infidels? In those circumstances, it would really be an argument of a man's want of spirit, of sense, and even of virtue to be a believer, because he would believe without sufficient evidence. Who would not, with every appearance of justice, suspect any cause, when he was not allowed to examine the arguments against it, and was only pressed with those in its favour?

What sensible and upright judge would decide a cause, where all the witnesses on one side were by violence prevented from giving their evidence? Those who converse with deists well know, that one of their strongest objections to christianity arises from hence, that none of the early writings against it are preserved. How much stronger, and even unanswerable, would that objection have been, if christianity had been, from the beginning, so effectually protected by the civil magistrate, that no person had dared to write against it at all. Such friends to the evidence and true interests of christianity, are all those who would suppress deistical writings at this day!

Suppose any article in a system of faith, so established and guarded, to be wrong, which is certainly a very modest supposition; let any of the advocates of this scheme say, how it is possible it should ever be rectified; or that, if the truth should insinuate itself, by any avenue which they had not sufficiently guarded, how it could bring its evidence along with it, so as to command the attention and acceptance which it deserved.

Indeed, it is not so much from the mistaken friends of truth that we apprehend these measures of rigid uniformity; but rather from those who would sacrifice truth, and every other consideration to public tranquility; from those MERE STATESMEN who, looking upon all systems of religion to be equally false, and not able to bear examination, will not suffer that examination to take place; for fear of destroying a system, which, however false, they imagine to be necessary to the peace and well being of the state. The most unrelenting persecution is to be apprehended, not from bigots, but from infidels. A bigot, who is so from a principle of conscience, may possibly be moved by a regard to the consciences of others; but the man who thinks that conscience ought always to be sacrificed to political views, has no principle on which an argument in favour of moderation can lay hold. Was not Bolingbroke the greatest promoter of the schism bill in England, and Richlieu of the persecution of the protestants in France?

Besides, as was, in some measure, observed before, all these systems of uniformity, in political or religious institutions, are the highest injustice to posterity. What natural right have we to judge for them, any more than our ancestors had to judge for us? Our ancestors, from the time of the Britons, had, no doubt, as high an opinion of their political and religious institutions as we can have of ours. But should we not have thought the fate of Great-Britain singularly unhappy, if they had been entailed upon us? and the very same reason of complaint will our posterity have, if we take any methods to perpetuate what we approve, as best for ourselves in our present circumstances; for farther than this we cannot pretend to see.

Let us, by all means, make our own circumstances as easy as possible; but let us lay posterity under no difficulty in improving theirs, if they see it convenient: rather, let all plans of policy be such as will easily admit of extension, and improvements of all kinds, and that the least violence, or difficulty of any kind, may attend the making of them. This is, at least, very desirable, and I believe it is far from being impracticable. However, though it should not be thought proper to unfix any thing which is at present established, let us proceed no farther than is manifestly necessary in those establishments.

Posterity, it may be said, will never complain of our institutions, when they have been educated in a strong and invincible attachment to them. It is true; and had we been pagans or papists, through a similar system of education, fixed in a more early period, we should not have complained. We, like the old Spartans, or the sons of bigotry in Spain and Portugal at present, might have been hugging our chains, and even proud of them. But other persons, who could have made a comparison between our actual condition, and what it would have been, had those institutions not been made, would have complained for us. They would have seen us to be a less great, wise, and happy people; which affords the same argument against throwing difficulties in the way of future improvements.

Highly as we think of the wisdom of our ancestors, we justly think ourselves, of the present age, wiser, and, if we be not blinded by the mere prejudice of education, must see, that we can, in many respects, improve upon the institutions they have transmitted to us. Let us not doubt, but that every generation in posterity will be as much superior to us in political, and in all kinds of knowledge, and that they will be able to improve upon the best civil and religious institutions that we can prescribe for them. Instead then of adding to the difficulties, which we ourselves find in making the improvements we wish to introduce, let us make this great and desirable work easier to them than it has been to us.

However, such is the progress of knowledge, and the enlargement of the human mind, that, in future time, notwithstanding all possible obstructions thrown in the way of human genius, men of great and exalted views will undoubtedly arise, who will see through and detest our narrow politics; when the ill-advisers and ill-advised authors of these illiberal and contracted schemes will be remembered with infamy and execration; and when, notwithstanding their talents as statesmen or writers, and though they may have pursued the same mind-enslaving schemes by more artful, and less sanguinary methods, they will be ranked among the Bonners and the Gardiners of past ages. They must be worse than Bonners and Gardiners, who could pursue the same ends by the same means, in this more humane and more enlightened age.

The time may come, when this country of Great-Britain shall lose her liberty. There are, who think they perceive too many symptoms of this approaching loss; but while the precious moments of freedom remain, let us, at least, indulge ourselves in the gloomy satisfaction of predicting the infamy, that will certainly overwhelm the authors of our servitude; whether they be future kings, and their tools the ministers, or ministers, and their tools the kings.

[Indeed, ministers are much more to be suspected of designs upon the liberties of a people than kings. For, in all arbitrary governments, it is the minister that is, in fact, possessed of the power of the state, the prince having nothing but the name, and the burdensome pageantry of it. Those princes, therefore, who listen to such pernicious advice, are, in reality, submitting their own necks, and those of their posterity, to the yoke of their servants. For, such is the condition of human affairs, that, in all the successions of arbitrary princes, *nine* have been weak, and governed by others, for *one* who has been able to govern himself; and in despotic monarchies, the chance of having able sovereigns is, on many accounts, much less than in others.]

This seems to be the time, when the minds of men are opening to large and generous views of things. Politics are more extended in practice, and better understood in theory. Religious knowledge is greatly advanced, and the principle of *universal toleration* is gaining ground apace. Schemes of ecclesiastical policy, which, in times of barbarity, ignorance, and superstition, were intimately interwoven with schemes of civil policy, and which, in fact, made the greatest part of the old political mixed constitution, have been gradually excluded; till, at present, though ecclesiastical power be looked upon as an useful support and auxiliary of civil government, it is pretty much detached from it. And the more sensible part of mankind are evidently in a progress to the belief, that ecclesiastical and civil jurisdiction, being things of a totally different nature, ought, if possible, to be wholly disengaged from one another. Religious sentiments, with respect to their influence on civil society, will perhaps be regarded, in time, as a theory of morals, only of a higher and more perfect kind, excellent to enforce a regard to magistracy, and the political duties, but improperly adopted into the same system and enforced by the same penalties. Till we know whether this work, which seems to be going forward in several parts of Europe, be of God, or not, let us not take, at least any rigid and violent methods to oppose it, but patiently wait the issue; unless, in the mean time, the disorders of the state absolutely force us into violent measures. At present, notwithstanding some trifling alarm, perhaps artfully raised and propagated, may seem to give a handle to the friends of arbitrary power to make use of some degree of coercion, more gentle measures seem better adapted to ensure tranquility.

England hath hitherto taken the lead in almost every thing great and good, and her citizens stand foremost in the annals of fame, as having shaken off the fetters which hung upon the human mind, and called it forth to the exertion of its noblest powers; and her constitution has been so far from receiving any injury from the efforts of these her free born enterprising sons, that she is, in part, indebted to them for the unrivalled reputation she now enjoys, of having the best system of policy in Europe. After weathering so many real storms, let us not quit the helm at the apprehension of imaginary dangers, but steadily hold on in what, I trust, is the most glorious course that a human government can be in. Let all the friends of liberty and human nature join to free the minds of men from the shackles of narrow and impolitic laws. Let us be free ourselves, and leave the blessings of freedom to our posterity.

[No nation ever was, or can be truly great, powerful, and happy by pursuing oppressive and persecuting measures. And a sovereign, who has a true sense of his present and future glory, must see it can only arise from his being the head of a great, powerful, and happy nation, made, or continued so, by himself. His best friends are those who would raise his greatness, by augmenting the greatness of the people over whom he presides. He himself must see the absurdity of every scheme which proposes to raise his character at the expense of that of his country; as if it were possible to depress the people to the condition of slaves, without sinking the sovereign into a master of such slaves. Poor preeminence! Such maxims may have influence with Asiatic monarchs, but can never impose on a sovereign of Great-Britain, educated in British principles, and with a just regard to the privileges of his subjects, with which his own true dignity is inseparably connected.

The nation will execrate, and the discerning prince will see through, and detest the meanness of that adulation, which, however disguised, would tend to enslave the kingdom, and debase the king. The meanest tool of the meanest party may exclaim against licentiousness and faction; men of genius, learning, and integrity, may, through the force of prejudice, be induced to join in the cry; and courtiers may think to recommend themselves to a sovereign by any measures which tend to quiet the clamours of the people; but the true enemy of sedition, and he who most effectually pays his court to a wise and good prince, is the man, who, without any views of preferment, proposes, with a manly freedom, whatever he thinks conducive to the greatness and glory of his country. This conduct cannot fail, both to give satisfaction to his fellow citizens, and ensure him the esteem of his prince; because such measures will proportionably raise the lustre of all ranks of men in the state, will make a wise prince the idol of a grateful nation, and endear his memory to the latest posterity.]

F I N I S.

127

The
Present State
Of
Liberty in Great Britain
and
Her Colonies.

Heu miseri cives, non Hostem, inimicaque castra, – Vestras Spes uritis.

VIRGIL.[1]

Preface.

It is of great importance, that all the subjects of government should have a just idea of their natural and civil rights, and that they should be apprized when they are invaded. As few of the pieces that I have seen on the subject of government in general, or concerning the attempts which have been made on the liberty of this country, are sufficiently plain and intelligible, I have endeavoured to supply the defect, by treating of these subjects in the way of *Questions and Answer*, which gives me an opportunity of touching the true state of the litigated points in the clearest manner.

I have not knowingly misrepresented any facts: the reflections I have made upon them are such as I could not avoid, and the liberty I have taken with the measures of government, is no greater than the constitution of this kingdom both admits and requires; any thing farther than this, is no concern of mine. I shall contentedly and cheerfully leave the issue to the merits of the cause, and to that good Providence which disposes of all things.

Sincerely do I deplore the infatuation of those who were the authors of the measures that I have animadverted upon, but more that of those who persist in carrying them on, notwithstanding their consequences are, every day, more and more alarming. In this I have a view, chiefly, to our late measures respecting *North America*, a case in which

---

'Heu miseri[ae] cives, non hostem, inimicaque castra, / [Argivum] – vestras spes uritis.'
['Whither now, whither are ye bound, ah! my wretched countrywomen? 'Tis not the foe, not the hostile Argive campe ye burn, but youre hopes.'] Virgil, *Aeniad*, V.671.

every man, woman, and child among us, and our posterity, to the latest generation, are deeply interested.

Pity it is, that the iron hand of oppression should be extended to those people, whom nothing but a love of freedom induced to leave their native clime, in the arbitrary reigns of our former princes! How preposterous is it, that those who glory in a free constitution for themselves, should wish for a power over *their fellow-subjects*, which would make them the most abject slaves, of which there is any account in history; that a commercial nation should take measures to cut off the greatest source of their own wealth; and that a nation which, on many accounts, stands in need of *peace*, should, in asserting her unjust claims, provoke a contest, which, if the Americans be the genuine offspring of Britons, cannot but be attended with the most pernicious consequences to both! Earnestly, therefore, must every friend to *Great Britain* and the *Colonies* (whose interest is the same) pray, that this dreadful and unnatural struggle may be prevented, by the success of their constitutional, loyal, and peaceable efforts for freedom, for securing their natural rights as men, and the civil rights which they have hitherto enjoyed as Englishmen.

Gladly would I indulge a more cheerful prospect, both with respect to *America* and *Great Britain*. The *tree of liberty*, I trust, has taken too deep root in both countries, not to be able to stand the shock of a few storms, before it be quite overturned. I hope it can be nothing more than a temporary delusion that we are permitted to labour under, and that the united voice of a loyal people, humbly petitioning for the security of their invaluable rights, will at length be heard. The *folly*, if not the *iniquity*, of all attempts to enslave a great and magnanimous nation, or any part of it, is surely too glaring not to be seen before they can be put in execution.

If, notwithstanding this, the time should be approaching (though I hope it is still at a great distance) when, as *Montesquieu* has prophesied, this country shall lose its liberty[2] yet, while the precious moments of freedom remain, let us, at least, indulge ourselves in the gloomy satisfaction of reviewing the infamy which has always sooner or later overwhelmed – the authors, or promoters, of their country's ruin – whether they were kings – and their tools the ministers, or (as I

---

[2] Montesquieu, *The Spirit of the Laws*, XI.6.

have shown to be in all cases more justly suspected) they were ministers, and their tools the kings.

In circumstances so discouraging, all the consolation we can have, must be derived from the consideration of the *unsearchable ways of Divine Providence*, and the gracious designs of that great Being, who can bring good out of the greatest seeming evil. And most earnestly do I pray, that he "who has the hearts of princes in his hands, and who turns them as rivers of water which way soever he pleases," may give those who have done wrong, understanding to see, and virtue to acknowledge their errors and injustice, that the spirit of discord, which seems to have gone forth among us, may be restrained; and that the present distractions of this country may issue in the real good of all its inhabitants.

For my own part, I cannot help saying, that if such measures as have for some time been adopted, continue to influence the British ministry, I shall make little account of my privileges as an Englishman, and, I trust, shall think more of those which are infinitely more valuable and less precarious, which I hope for as a Christian and a citizen of heaven.

The
Present State of Liberty,
&c.

SECTION I.

Of Government in general.

Question. WHAT is a *society? Answer.* A *society* consists of a number of persons united by their common interest, and by the use of the same measures to promote that interest.

Q. What are the advantages of society? A. Without the aid of society, a single person would not, in many cases, be able to procure a redress of his grievances, or many of the conveniences of life, both of which may be accomplished by the wisdom and strength of a whole community. Biased by a regard to their separate interests, men, unconnected with society, would think differently concerning their own rights, and those of their neighbours, and there being no persons to whom an appeal could be made, the dispute would either terminate in violence and blood, or the weaker must yield to the imposition and oppression of the stronger.

Q. Who are the *supreme magistrates* of a state? A. *Supreme magistrates* are those persons who act in the name of, and for the public, in those cases in which it would be impossible or inconvenient for all the members of the society to assemble and act for themselves.

Q. How far does the power of the supreme magistrates extend? A. As the supreme magistrates represent the whole society, their power is the same with that of the society itself; and the good of the society being the great object and end of their union, the magistrates have the same power of doing every thing which they think conducive to that end, that the people themselves would have, if they could be assembled for that purpose.

Q. Are the supreme magistrates, then, subject to no control whatever? A. The supreme magistrates being appointed by the people, in order to do their business, they are necessarily to be considered as *the servants of the people*, who have, therefore, a right to call them to account, if they do not answer the great ends for which they were appointed.

Q. What things should the public laws, or the regulations of the supreme magistrates, respect? A. As the end of society, and consequently of the institution of magistracy, is *the good of the whole body*; laws, or public regulations, should respect those things only in which the wisdom and strength of the society can be exerted to the advantage of the members of it.

Q. Is it not better, in all cases, to have recourse to the wisdom and strength of the whole, than to depend upon the prudence and force of individuals? A. No, there are many cases in which this interference of magistracy would produce the greatest confusion, embarrassment, and distress; as, for instance, if the magistrates should forbid parents to punish their children, or their servants, and take the whole business of correction upon themselves; if they should prescribe what medicines should be taken in particular disorders, or appoint the physicians, to whose prescriptions we should, in all cases, be obliged to conform; or if they should dictate to us the object or mode of our religious worship, which respects our happiness not in this, but in a future state.

Q. Does not every person, when he becomes a member of society, virtually surrender the power which he before enjoyed, of providing for his own security and happiness? A. He does so; but only with respect to those things in which the public can make better provision for them than he could for himself; because the good of the whole requires this, and nothing more. Any power, therefore, which magistrates assume, farther than this, is tyranny, and an arbitrary invasion of men's natural rights.

Q. What is the best security of these natural rights? A. The great natural rights and liberties of mankind are best secured when the supreme magistracy is in the hands of persons chosen by the people, and when they are entrusted with that power for a limited time. For, if once the supreme magistracy fall into the hands of persons who are independent of the people, they may fancy that they have an interest separate from that of the people, in which case they will naturally usurp the rights of the people, and aggrandize themselves at their expense.

Q. Is it necessary that all the people should have voices in the election of their supreme magistrates? A. No, it will generally be sufficient if the choice of magistrates be in the majority of those whose circumstances render them above being corrupted, so as to give their voices in an improper manner. For when persons of this class provide for their own interest, they will necessarily provide for that of the society at large.

Q. What is the first step that the people should take when they are oppressed by their governors, being either deprived of their natural rights, or of the only sure guard of them, the choice of their magistrates? A. They must make strong remonstrances to those governors who have betrayed their trust, expressing their sense of the injustice that has been done them, and their abhorrence of the maxims of government, by which they have been oppressed.

Q. May a people go no farther than this, in order to obtain a redress of national grievances? A. In general, this will be sufficient; for no person, who is not entirely divested of the common feelings of mankind, will bear to live abhorred by his fellow-citizens, and to die with infamy entailed upon his name and posterity. But if, through the infatuation of governors, intoxicated with power, these means should be insufficient to obtain the end, nothing hinders that people, thus grossly abused and insulted by their magistrates, (who, by whatever name they are distinguished, are, in fact, nothing more than their servants,) should strip them of their power, and confer it where they have reason to hope it will be less abused. It was this principle which justified and effected the glorious Revolution, and gave our forefathers a happy relief from the tyranny and oppressions of *James* II.

Q. In what countries is it most difficult to oppose the attempts of tyrannical magistrates? A. In countries of great extent, in which the people live at a great distance from one another, so that they can never assemble, or by any other means act in concert, and combine against their tyrants; and where also the magistrates must necessarily be intrusted with great power, and have a great number of officers under them, who will generally be attached to their interest, and support their measures, be they ever so villainous and oppressive. So great are the advantages of which the sovereign is possessed in these circumstances, that there are few countries in the world, of considerable extent, which are not at this day in a state of actual slavery, the people having no power of arriving at the supreme magistracy themselves, or votes in the nomination of those magistrates. If the natural rights of those people are, in any measure, preserved, it is because the prince does not think it worth his while to molest them, or because the spirit and customs of the times have given them a sanction, which he hath not the courage to violate. Abject slaves as the *Turks* are, they have many privileges which the grand *Seignior*[3] dares not invade.

Q. Whether are kings or ministers more justly suspected of designs upon the liberties of a people? A. In general, the ministers: for in all arbitrary governments, it is the minister who is, in fact, possessed of the chief power of the state, while the prince has nothing but the name and the pageantry of it. Those princes, therefore, who listen to their pernicious advice, are, in reality, submitting their own necks, and those of their posterity, to the yoke of their servants. For such is the condition of human affairs, that, in all successions of sovereign princes, *nine* have been weak, and governed by others, for *one* who has been able to govern himself. Indeed, in arbitrary monarchies, the chance of having able princes is, on many accounts, much less than in other states.

[3] The Ottoman Sultan.

SECTION II.

Of the State of Liberty in England.

Q. What are the outlines of the constitution of Great Britain? A. Great Britain is a country in which the supreme magistracy is lodged in the three estates of the realm; one of which is the *King*, and is hereditary; another the House of *Lords*, who are such, either by inheritance, or the king's pleasure; and the third is the House of *Commons*, who (though imperfectly and unequally) represent the people.

Q. What is meant by the *king's prerogative?* A. The king's prerogative is by no means a discretionary power of doing what he thinks to be right, in things that are not expressly provided for by law. The prerogative is a branch of the common law of the land, enabling the king to do those acts only which it has been customary for the king to perform, and, like any other article of common law, is to be ascertained by precedent. It would be no free government, if any thing was excepted from the jurisdiction of law, and submitted to the determination of arbitrary pleasure.

Q. How is it said that the king can do no wrong? A. The meaning of it is, that the king is not personally responsible for any measures of government, but the ministers who advised them. It is essential to the freedom of government, that all public measures should be imputed to persons who may be freely censured, and arraigned at the bar of the public. For if it were once admitted, that the king himself engaged in any public measures, of his own motion, since it is an allowed maxim that he can do no wrong, there could be no redress of grievances. It is absolutely and obviously necessary, that a person who must not be supposed to do wrong, should never be supposed to do any thing.

Q. Where lies the security which the bulk of the people enjoy for the continuance of their natural and civil rights? A. In the House of Commons, who are chosen by themselves; for the lords, whose number is filled up at the pleasure of the king, and who must live in splendour, and whose younger sons and numerous dependents must be provided for by the court, may be expected to be, in general, in the interest of the court.

Q. What is it that the people of England have most to fear, as being most liable to subject them to arbitrary power? A. The corruption of their representatives; for when once it shall be in the power of the court to secure, by places or pensions, a majority in the House of Commons, that house will no longer represent the sentiments of the people, but the pleasure of the king only. And then this important branch of the legislature will not only become insignificant, with respect to its original intention, but will be the most dangerous engine of oppression; *Britons*, like the *Romans* under the emperors, will be enslaved, with all the external badges of freedom.

Q. What are the circumstances respecting the House of Commons, which give thinking men the most reason to apprehend, that we are approaching to this dreadful situation? A. The great number of placemen and pensioners, and of those who are in expectation of emoluments of that kind, in that house. These never fail to second the measures of the administration, whatever they are. To this is added, the long continuance of their power, viz. for *seven years*, which was originally an arbitrary usurpation of the rights of the people, and which makes it worth their while to lay out great sums of money to secure a seat, which, in such a number of years, is sure to afford them an opportunity of reimbursing themselves with advantage.

Q. How comes it to pass, that it is in the power of the court to get so many of their partisans into the house, when the members of it represent the people, and are elected by them? A. It arises from so great a majority of the members being chosen by the inhabitants, or freemen of inconsiderable towns, the sole property of which is in the hands of some of the lords, or other adherents to the court, who can oblige them to return whoever they shall direct.[4]

Q. As you seemed to represent our *political rights*, as of use only to guard our *natural and civil rights*, and that, in some cases, these are sufficiently guarded by the spirit of the times, and other circumstances that control a tendency to despotism, notwithstanding the people have no share in the legislature; are we so happy as to have no

[4] Referring to the repeated annulment of Wilkes' electoral victory as Member of Parliament for Middlesex.

137

reason to apprehend any thing from the loss of our political liberty? Do the persons who are in administration seem disposed to make any attempts upon our privileges as men and Englishmen? A. The ministry of Great Britain have, of late years, made many alarming attacks upon the essential rights and privileges of the subject; and there is not, as yet, any prospect of their being called to account for their illegal and arbitrary proceedings.

Q. What are the great privileges of Englishmen, which have been infringed by them? A. 1. They have evaded the operation of the great writ of *Habeas Corpus*, whereby a person accused of any crime cannot be detained in custody, but must be brought immediately to a court of law, and be admitted to bail (if the offence be of such a nature as to be bailable) till he can be tried according to law. 2. They have, by a *general warrant*, in which no person was said to have been accused upon oath, or so much as named, arrested the person of an Englishman, and a member of the House of Commons, removing him from the custody of one person to that of another, and confined him, without admitting his nearest friends to speak to him. By the same warrant they seized all his private *papers*, and out of them, thus illegally procured, collected evidence for a crime, which supposes that he himself published those papers. 3. They restrict the liberty of the press, that great security for every other branch of our liberty, and the scourge of their arbitrary proceedings, by construing all censures upon them, and their measures, into *libels*, and procuring the authors of them to be severely punished. 4. They have, in these cases of libels, contrived to evade the great privilege of Englishmen, that of being tried by their peers, in the method of *jury*, not daring to trust the issue of such base prosecutions to the impartial judgement of their countrymen; and, in the place of it, they have extended the methods of trial by *attachment, information*, and *interrogatories*, in which juries are not used, and which are conducted in a manner as unfavourable to liberty, as the Inquisition in the Church of Rome, and the odious Star-chamber under the *Stuarts*. 5. The great *Bill of Rights* has been invaded by a repeated refusal, to admit the first county in England, to judge of the fitness of the person who shall represent them in parliament; and one whom they had freely chosen has been excluded, though guilty of no crime that was not publicly known at the time of election, and none for which the law had not had its full satisfaction.

6. Recourse has unnecessarily been had to that great engine of arbitrary power, *a military force*, in a manner contrary to the genius and spirit of our constitution.

Q. What can the people do in such a situation of their affairs, when their most valuable rights seem to be in danger? A. In these circumstances every man, who wishes well to his country, should contribute liberally to the support of all that suffer in the common cause of liberty, and spread the alarm through the whole kingdom, in order to make all the people thoroughly sensible of the impending danger. They must promote the sending of instructions to members of parliament, from all the free and independent electors, expressing their sentiments of the state of public affairs, and to get petitions for the redress of grievances, signed by all ranks and orders of men, who are unbiased by court preferment, and have no expectations from that quarter, for themselves, or their friends. And there can be no doubt, but that the voice of the nation, rendered thus clear and audible, will be heard. No minister could bear to live in a country, in which he should see himself abhorred by all men of sense and virtue. The truth would, at length, reach the ear of our most gracious sovereign. He would listen to the reasonable requests of his loyal subjects. Both would again be happy in their mutual affection. Then affairs would be established by concord at home, and then no power on earth would dare to provoke their resentment.

Q. What should be the immediate object of the friends of this country at this time, and what should be the principal articles in their instructions to their representatives in parliament? A. As the foundation of all the preceding disorders, all placemen, court-pensioners, and sons of the nobility, should be excluded the House of Commons. The duration of the present, and of all future parliaments, should be shortened; and, if possible, the small boroughs should be abolished; and all the members should be elected in some such manner as by counties. Also the candidates should take the oath against bribery and corruption, and the election should be by ballot. Were these essential points once gained, all the rest would follow of course. Impeachments would be preferred against all those who should advise tyrannical and oppressive measures, and subsequent ministers would be deterred, by their punishment, from following their example. But if, in our present circumstances, the full establishment of our rights, for the future, could be procured, it would be well worth while to purchase it by an *act of indemnity*, and the oblivion of every thing that has hitherto been done in violation of them.

SECTION III.

Of the Affairs of America.

Q. Have the members of the present administration extended their arbitrary measures beyond the bounds of Great Britain? A. Yes, they are pursuing measures still more arbitrary and oppressive with the inhabitants of North America.

Q. What is the great grievance that those people complain of? A. It is their being taxed by the parliament of Great Britain, the members of which are so far from taxing themselves, that they ease themselves at the same time. If this measure takes place, the colonists will be reduced to a state of as complete servitude, as any people of which there is an account in history. For by the same power, by which the people of England can compel them to pay *one penny*, they may compel them to pay the *last penny* they have.[5] There will be nothing but arbitrary imposition on the one side, and humble petition on the other.

Q. Have not the people of North America been greatly benefited by the English? Was not the late expensive war undertaken on their account, and is it not reasonable that they should, at least, bear their

---

[5] Though the infamous Stamp Act (1765) was repealed one year later, the same fears were aroused by the promulgation of the Townshend Acts (1768). These imposed a series of import fees and intensified customs duties designed to support governors and judges in the colonies independent of grants from colonial legislatures.

share of the burden of it? A. This is an argument very proper to be urged with the colonists, in case they should refuse to assist their mother-country, but it is well known that, besides bearing very heavy taxes, imposed by their own houses of assembly, for the support of their own government, they have always been ready, of their own accord, to serve the common cause to the utmost of their ability, and, as some have thought, even beyond it. But admitting they had not done this, is not absolute slavery too great a punishment for their ingratitude?

Q. Are there not many considerable towns in England, as *Leeds and Manchester*, which send no representatives to parliament, and yet, notwithstanding this, are taxed by them? What have the Americans to complain of more? A. The representation of this country in parliament is acknowledged to be very unequal and imperfect; but the effect of this imperfection and inequality of representation, is of little consequence, so long as the persons who impose the tax upon others, impose it upon themselves at the same time; for if they feel nothing for others, they will feel for themselves. A parallel to the present case of the Americans, would be a tax upon those towns who send no representatives, or an exemption of those towns who send no representatives, or an exemption of those towns that do send members. In this case, would not *Leeds* and *Manchester* make as loud complaints as the people of North America do now? Would any motive, but that arising from the want of power, prevent their resisting the levying of such a tax, notwithstanding it should be passed into a bill, in the most regular and authentic manner, by all the three estates of the realm?

Q. Hath it not been the custom, in former times at least, for the English parliament to impose taxes on those provinces which sent no members to it? A. By no means. *Ireland*, though a conquered country, always taxed itself, and doth so to this day. The king of England never does more than lay his wants before the Irish parliament, and receives what they themselves think proper to give him. The *Scots*, also, taxed themselves before the Union. Wales, a conquered country, did the same, and even the inhabitants of the counties palatine, before they, at their own request, sent members to represent them in the English House of Commons.

Q. Does not the British parliament make laws that restrict the commerce of the colonies, and may not this burden be equivalent to a tax? A. The British parliament also makes laws that restrict the commerce of *Ireland*, but notwithstanding the near neighbourhood of this country, whereby we are pretty good judges of its circumstances, we never presumed to lay a direct tax upon it, nor indeed upon *North America*, till of late. Allowing that, eventually, there is no difference between these things, the one is a much more open and undisguised oppression than the other; and there is a degree to which any people will bear hardship without complaint; but oppression, beyond a certain degree, will make even a wise man mad. Such powers as, from their nature, must necessarily be lodged in one of the parts of the whole empire, the Colonists will never object to in Great Britain. The most absolute jurisdiction of this kind they would never complain of; and, provided the effects of it were not greatly oppressive, they would never think of nicely setting bounds to it. It may, perhaps, be impossible (if the subject be metaphysically considered) to fix precise boundaries to the authority of Great Britain over the Colonies, but the extremes, in a thousand cases of great importance, (as in all questions concerning morals, virtue, and vice,) may be obvious, when the exact medium cannot be ascertained; and, in this case, moderation on both sides would make that very easy in practice, which is ever so difficult in theory.

Q. What can the *North Americans* plead for an exemption from taxes imposed by the British parliament, but such *charters* as our kings have usually given to corporations, which are all of them liable to be regulated, or set aside by all the three estates of the realm? A. Admitting that the privileges of the *Colonists* had no other origin, yet the continuance of this establishment such a number of years, and the fatal consequence of revoking it, which is nothing less than the absolute slavery of a whole people, ought to make their rights to be considered in a very different light from that of the charters of common corporations, the members of which are generally benefited by their abrogation. A corporate town generally bears a very small proportion to the whole state; whereas all our *North American* Colonies bear a very great proportion to the whole, and, in all probability, will, at no great distance of time, be equal to all the rest put together. And it ought not to be forgotten, that it is the good of *the whole empire*, considered as one, which should be the object of government, and not the aggrandizement of any particular part. If other maxims prevail, one part of the empire will be the seat of despotism, and all the other subjects will be slaves.

Q. In all disputes between *Great Britain* and her *Colonies*, must not Great Britain, though she be only one part of the whole united empire, be, of necessity, the judge; and should not the Colonies, therefore, submit to her decision? Who can be umpire between them? A. It is true, things are so circumstanced, that, in all disputes, *Great Britain* must, of course, be the judge; because she has the power of enforcing the sentence; but she cannot act in that capacity, contrary to the clear sense of the Colonies, without asserting an undisguised tyranny and arbitrary power. Though Great Britain be the stronger of the two, she should let *reason* be judge between them, and not take advantage of more strength, to oppress those who are not able to resist her unjust decrees. If (to recur to the case I put before) the parliament of Great Britain should lay a tax upon Leeds, Manchester, or any other town, that sends no representatives to parliament; or if the three estates should concur to deprive any particular subject of his natural and civil rights, (for instance, his right of being elected to serve his country in parliament,) in this case Great Britain would likewise assume the office of judge. There could be no appeal from the sentence, and the town, or the individual, would submit; but they would give way as they would to a tempest, a torrent, or a hurricane, which they were not able to resist, and they would relieve themselves the first opportunity.

Q. But is not the advantage accruing to Great Britain from this taxation of America, a plausible pretence for having recourse to so oppressive a measure? A. By no means. The acquisition by taxes is, and always will be, inconsiderable, and is infinitely overbalanced by the *loss of trade*, arising from the disaffection of the Colonies to their mother country, and their consequent aversion to take our commodities.

Q. What is supposed to be the amount of our trade to our Colonies? A. I think I have heard it computed at about one-fourth of our whole commerce; and provided the inhabitants of North America multiply as they have done hitherto, (and there is a prospect of their increasing even faster, as they have now more room to extend themselves, without fear of the French,) in less than a century, it will not be in the power of Great Britain to supply their demand for manufactures, were all her inhabitants employed in them.

Q. But will not the Colonists choose to manufacture for themselves? A. It is far from being their interest to commence manufacturers, and nothing but necessity can drive them to it. Land is so cheap, that every man is ambitious of acquiring property in it. Few hands, therefore, being at liberty to apply to labour or manufactures, their work is so dear, that it will always be for their interest to purchase of us, rather than supply themselves, till the whole country be fully peopled, which is a period too remote for attention.

Q. What seem to be the best, the most equitable, and advantageous maxims to be observed by Great Britain with respect to our Colonies? A. The most equitable maxims, as well as the best policy, in our conduct to the Americans, is to lay aside all jealousy of them, not to indulge the idea of superiority, and to consult the good of the whole, as of one united empire, each part of which has the same natural right to liberty and happiness with the other, to encourage agriculture among them, and manufactures among ourselves, and by no means interfere in their interior government, so far as to lay any tax upon them, either for the purpose of raising a revenue, or for any other purpose whatever. The benefits arising *spontaneously* from our extensive and increasing commerce with them, will infinitely overbalance all that we shall ever be able to extort from them by way of *tax*. Thus shall we be mutually the source of strength and opulence to each other, and nothing, in the ordinary course of Divine Providence, but a wrong-headed and tyrannical administration, can hinder our being the most flourishing and the happiest state upon the face of the earth.

Q. But have we not gone too far to recede, without coming to extremities? A. It is never too late for any man, or body of men, to repent of, and rectify, what they are convinced they have done amiss. Let us, at least, virtually acknowledge it, by generously cancelling all that is past, and suffering things to remain for the future as they were some years ago. (Happy years of mutual love and confidence!) This will not fail to secure the gratitude and affection of the Colonists. Nay, more, having seen our errors, and repented of them, there will be a better foundation laid for mutual confidence than ever.

Amantium iræ amoris redintegratio est.[6]

[6]'Lovers' quarrels are love's renewal' (Terence, *Lady of Andros*, III. 556).

Index

America, North xiii, xvii, 9, 84, 89, 129, 140, 142
atheism xxvi, 57, 59, 66
Athens xix, 40, 45, 49, 109
authority 43, 46, 65, 73, 87, 91, 94, 104, 115, 117

Balguy, Thomas 3, 73–4, 91, 95, 98, 101, 102–3
Bentham, Jeremy xiv
Blackburne, Francis (*The Confessional*) xxvii, 5, 102, 106, 115
Blackstone, William xxii, xxiii
Brown, John xvii, xviii, xix, xxv, 1, 40, 48, 57, 59, 108, 110, 117–18
Burgh, James xiv, xvi, xviii

Canada xii
Cartwright, John xiv, xviii, xxiv
Charles I xi, 22
Charles II 22
Church of England (establishment) xi, xiii, xx, xxiii, 5, 7, 54, 61, 68, 73–4, 83–7, 89, 99, 107, 111, 113–14, 122
civil society 46–7, 50, 53, 55, 108, 111–12
Clarke, Samuel xv, 114, 119
colonies xii, 143
commerce 84, 130, 142–4
common good, public good xii–xiii, xviii, xxi–xxii, 11, 13–14, 17, 23, 26, 31, 52, 56, 76, 133, 144
Commonwealth xi

'commonwealth' xix
'Commonwealthmen' xii
community xii, xiii–xix, xxi, xxv, 11–12, 17, 31–2, 46, 49, 88
consent xiii, xiv, 13

dependence 15, 30
despotism *see* tyranny
Dissenters xiii, xxii, 6, 52, 65, 88, 90, 92, 98, 101, 105, 116, 122

education 39–40, 42, 45, 50–2, 124
Egypt 109
empire xi, xii, xiii, 144
enlightenment xxii
enquiry (free) xix–xxiv, xxvii, 65–6, 93, 114, 118–19, 121
establishment *see* Church of England
equality xxiv, xxv, 13

France 33, 35, 48, 54, 63, 100
Franklin, Benjamin xv
freedom of thought *see* enquiry (free)
French Revolution xi

Galileo 37
gardening 44
Great Britain xi–xii, 21, 48, 51, 124, 125, 130, 143
Grotius xxv

happiness 14, 31, 39, 45–6, 53, 56, 82, 110–12, 134, 144
Hartley, David xvi
Hoadley, Benjamin 114, 119
Hutcheson 119

145

improvement (progress) xx, 9–10, 19,
    43–5, 106, 109, 112, 117, 119,
    125
independence 15, 36
India xii
individuals xviii, xxi, xxv, 30, 39, 45,
    64, 133
interests 16, 26, 32, 38, 46, 52, 57,
    76, 85, 95, 100, 122, 132, 144
Ireland 141, 142
Islam *see* Mahometan

James I 75
James II xi, 22, 135
Jesuits (resistance theory) 19
Jew, Jewish 48, 65, 67, 79, 80, 120

Kant, Immanuel xxvii
latitudinarian Anglicans xiii
liberty xvi, 4, 12, 44, 116, 122, 130,
    139, 144
    civil xxiv, xxv, 3, 12, 28, 32, 35,
        39–40
    intellectual xxi, xxiii, 44, 58
    political xxiv, 3, 12, 16, 28, 32, 35
    press 118, 138
Locke, John xxi, xxv, 3, 49, 60, 114,
    118

Mahometan 65, 74, 84
manners 42
Montesquieu 130

Newton, Isaac xv, 118
non-resistance *see* passive obedience

Parliament xi, xii, 16, 25, 34, 51, 74,
    137
    danger of corruption 137
    reform of 16, 35, 139, 143
passive obedience 19, 20, 66, 81, 104
patriotism xii, xix, 21
persecution 69, 81
Poland 54, 62n, 63
Pope, Alexander 29
popish inquisition *see* Roman
    Catholicism
prerogative 136
Price, Richard xiv, xvi, xviii, xiv
Priestley, Joseph xiv, xv, xxii
    An Address . . . to Dissenters xxii

*A Course of Lectures on the Theory of
    Language* xx
*Essay on the First Principles of
    Government* xiv, xvii, xviii, xx
*An Essay on a Course of Liberal
    Education* xvii, xx
*A Free Discussion of . . . Materialism
    and Philosophical Necessity* xvi
*The Importance and Extent of Free
    Inquiry in Matters of Religion: A
    Sermon* xxiv
*Institutes of Natural and Revealed
    Religion* xvi
*Lectures on History and General
    Policy* xxv
*A Letter of Advice to Protestant
    Dissenters* xxvi
Observations on Man xvi
*The Present State of Liberty in Great
    Britain and her Colonies* xvii, xxi
*Remarks on . . . Dr Blackstone's
    "Commentaries"* xxiii
*A View of the Principles and Conduct
    of the Protestant Dissenters* xxii,
    xxvii
private judgment xxii, xxvii, 11, 66,
    78, 101
progress *see* improvement
property 25, 29, 33–4
Protestant Reformation xx, 114, 115
Protestants xxii, 51, 60, 65, 66

rank 15, 16
reason xxi, xxvii, 11, 43, 45, 56
rebellion 20, 22, 27
religion 39, 52, 55, 64, 117
representation xiii, 11, 31, 141
republicanism xx, xxiv, 24, 40
resistance xi, 13, 16, 18–22, 25–6,
    134
Revolution of 1688 xi, 135
rights (natural or civil) xix, xxiv, xxvi,
    xxvii, 13, 22, 24, 31, 38, 46–7,
    56, 101, 129–30, 134, 136–37,
    144
    of Englishmen 21, 138
Roman Catholicism 48, 54, 61–2,
    65–6, 70, 73, 86, 89, 94, 104,
    116, 122
Rome (ancient) 41, 70, 79, 86, 110
Rousseau, Jean-Jacques 11

Index

Russell, William 23

salus populi suprema est lex [sic] 23
security xxi, xxii, xxiv, xxvi, 29, 32,
   36, 40, 97, 117, 134, 136
Seven Years War xii
Sidney, Algernon 23
size (of the polity) 11, 14, 21, 25
slavery 17, 34, 127
Socinian xiv
sovereignty xi
Sparta xix, 40–1, 45, 47, 109–10,
   124
state of nature 9
subscription *see* Thirty-Nine Articles

taxation xii, 17, 25, 89, 140, 142
Test and Corporation Acts xiii
Thirty-Nine Articles (subscription
   to) xiii, xvii, 87–8, 93, 116–17
toleration xi, xvii, xxi, xxvi, 54, 60,
   88, 102, 126

'True Whigs' xii
truth xxiii, xxvii, 4, 6, 30, 57, 66, 76,
   82, 116, 118–19, 122
Turkey 33, 37, 54, 135
tyranny xxii, 13, 17, 26, 28, 35, 37,
   50, 51, 62, 93, 112, 134–5

uniformity xiv, xxvi, 45, 95, 119, 123,
   124
Unitarian *see* Socinian
utilitarianism xviii, 65, 76, 81, 82

voting 15, 34, 42, 134, 139

Warburton, William (*Alliance Between
   Church and State*) xxiii, 4, 55, 61,
   74, 76, 82–3, 85, 88, 98, 103,
   106, 119
Wedgwood, Josiah xv
Whigs xii
William and Mary xi

147

Cambridge Texts in the History of Political Thought

Titles published in the series thus far

Aristotle *The Politics* (edited by Stephen Everson)

Arnold *Culture and Anarchy and Other Writings* (edited by Stefan Collini)

Bakunin *Statism and Anarchy* (edited by Marshall Shatz)

Bentham *A Fragment on Government* (introduction by Ross Harrison)

Bernstein *The Preconditions of Socialism* (edited by Henry Tudor)

Bodin *On Sovereignty* (edited by Julian H. Franklin)

Bossuet *Politics Drawn from the Very Words of Holy Scripture* (edited by Patrick Riley)

Burke *Pre-Revolutionary Writings* (edited by Ian Harris)

Cicero *On Duties* (edited by M. T. Griffin and E. M. Atkins)

Constant *Political Writings* (edited by Biancamaria Fontana)

Diderot *Political Writings* (edited by John Hope Mason and Robert Wokler)

The Dutch Revolt (edited by Martin van Gelderen)

Filmer *Patriarcha and Other Writings* (edited by Johann P. Sommerville)

Harrington *The Commonwealth of Oceana* and *A System of Politics* (edited by J. G. A. Pocock)

Hegel *Elements of the Philosophy of Right* (edited by Allen W. Wood and H. B. Nisbet)

Hobbes *Leviathan* (edited by Richard Tuck)

Hooker *Of the Laws of Ecclesiastical Polity* (edited by A. S. McGrade)

John of Salisbury *Policraticus* (edited by Cary Nederman)

Kant *Political Writings* (edited by H. S. Reiss and H. B. Nisbet)

Lawson *Politica sacra et civilis* (edited by Conal Condren)

Leibniz *Political Writings* (edited by Patrick Riley)

Locke *Two Treatises of Government* (edited by Peter Laslett)

Luther and Calvin on Secular Authority (edited by Harro Höpfl)

Machiavelli *The Prince* (edited by Quentin Skinner and Russell Price)

Malthus *An Essay on the Principle of Population* (edited by Donald Winch)

James Mill *Political Writings* (edited by Terence Ball)

J. S. Mill *On Liberty*, with *The Subjection of Women* and *Chapters on Socialism* (edited by Stefan Collini)

Milton *Political Writings* (edited by Martin Dzelzainis)

Montesquieu *The Spirit of the Laws* (edited by Anne M. Cohler, Basia Carolyn Miller and Harold Samuel Stone)

More *Utopia* (edited by George M. Logan and Robert M. Adams)

Nicholas of Cusa *The Catholic Concordance* (edited by Paul E. Sigmund)

Paine *Political Writings* (edited by Bruce Kuklick)

Price *Political Writings* (edited by D. O. Thomas)

Priestley *Political Writings* (edited by Peter N. Miller)

Proudhon *What is Property?* (edited by Donald R. Kelley and Bonnie G. Smith)

Pufendorf *On the Duty of Man and Citizen according to Natural Law* (edited by James Tully)

The Radical Reformation (edited by Michael G. Baylor)

Vitoria *Political Writings* (edited by Anthony Pagden and Jeremy Lawrance)

William of Ockham *A Short Discourse on Tyrannical Government* (edited by A. S. McGrade and John Kilcullen)

For EU product safety concerns, contact us at Calle de José Abascal, 56–1°,
28003 Madrid, Spain or eugpsr@cambridge.org.

 www.ingramcontent.com/pod-product-compliance
Ingram Content Group UK Ltd.
Pitfield, Milton Keynes, MK11 3LW, UK
UKHW012343130625
459647UK00009B/504